Conversations with Psyche

A Dreamer's Guide to Soul-Stirring Creativity

Artwork and illustrations by Victoria Rabinowe

Additional graphics by Sean Wells seanwellscreates@gmail.com

Copyright © 2024 by Victoria Rabinowe

All Rights Reserved. No part of this book may be reproduced or transmitted in any form or by any means, electronic or mechanical, including photocopying, recording, or by any information storage and retrieval system, without permission in writing from the publisher.

First edition
ISBN 978-0-9819045-2-8
Library of Congress Cataloguing in Publication Data
Rabinowe, Victoria, 1949-
Conversations with Psyche: A Dreamer's Guide to Soul-Stirring Creativity
written and illustrated by Victoria Rabinowe
Cm.
ISBN 978-0-9819045-2-8
1. Dreams. 2. Creativity. 3. Self-Help. 4. Psychology. 5. Diaries. 6. Art Journals. 7. Art Techniques. 8. Dream Interpretation. 9. Symbolism.
In this book, original or copyrighted images may have been incorporated into my illustrations as examples of synchronicity of the found image. My artwork examples are not for sale.
Calligraphy on the cover by Judythe Sieck. judythe.sieck@comcast.net
German translation by Janina Pollak and Johanna Vedral. johanna.vedral@gmail.com
Spanish translation by Elizabeth Garay garayliz@gmail.com
Italian language translation by Marzia Bosoni marzia.bosoni@gmail.com
Book Design by BadDog Design baddogdesign.biz

Published by Bright Shadow Press
www.VictoriaDreams.com
1432 Don Gaspar
Santa Fe, NM 87505 U.S.A.

A banquet is spread before us every night in our dreams if only we dare to partake.
—Marion Woodman

Dedication

Dedicated to the memory of my teacher, William Corbett, who introduced me to metaphor, innuendo, allegory and paradox.

CONTENTS

Genius of the Night Mind 13

Duende 15

Introduction 17

Invitation 25

PART I ABOUT DREAMS 37

A Separate Reality

My Process, My Practice

PART II THE MUSE IN THE NIGHT 59

The Encounter

The Conversation Dreams

PART III CAPTURE YOUR DREAMS 101

The Dream Journal

Getting Started

Dream Lexicon

Anatomy of the Dream

    Dream Characters

    Dream Creatures

    Dream Objects

    Dream Actions

    DreamScapes

    Questions

    Emotions

    Memories

PART IV DREAM JOURNAL TECHNIQUES 133

1 DreamWriting

    The Five Senses

    A Letter

    Harangue

    Deconstruction and Reconstruction

2 DreamPoetry

    Free Verse

    BlackOut Poetry

    List Poem

    Ode

    Limerick

    Pantoum

    Haiku

    Ballad

    Ditty

    Lampoon

    Found Poetry

3 DreamingArts

    Storyboard

    Zoom In / Zoom Out

    Mandala

    Collage

    Dream Map

    Diorama

    Mask

    Painting

4 DreamTheater
   Monologue
   Dialogue
   Campfire Story
   Screenplay
   Song
   Melodrama
   Body and Soul
   Stage the Dream

5 DreamJourneys
   Fairy Tale
   Board Game
   Comic Strip
   Alice in Dreamland
   Mythic Journey
   Child's Play
   Honor Bound
   Portrait of Power
   Pandora's Dream Box
   Pearl of Great Price
   Witches' Brew
   A New Ending
   Labyrinth
   Sanctuary
   Utopian Vision
   Prayer

Guidelines For Dream Groups. . . . 208

PART V THE ART OF
ONE DREAM 213

AFTERWORD
The Inner Journey 308

EPILOGUE
Source of Creativity 310

APPENDIX A
Ethics Statement 312

APPENDIX B
DreamingArts as a Therapeutic
Tool for Psychotherapy. 313

APPENDIX C
Resource List for
Further Reading 314

Genius of the Night Mind

The most beautiful thing we can experience is the mysterious.
—Albert Einstein

Your night mind is a gateway to an unfathomably vast universe. This book offers a way to traverse the unknown topography of the mind, investigating the mystery of existence, opening the door to imagination, magic, awe and grace, where the soul-centered life meets Psyche in an evocative and endlessly generative conversation.

Wherefrom, man of god?
What outrageous fate has led you here?
You seduced me with your accursed curiosity,
desirously stretching my hand after divine mysteries.
—C.G. Jung

Duende

Dreams express themselves with Duende—the fiery spirit that stirs the emotions with a mysterious power that humans feel but no philosopher can explain. Duende speaks with the language of the blood in all its many aspects: desperate, ruinous, tormented; rapturous, defiant, transcendent. When you dare to dig deep into the marrow of your dreams, you will inevitably pull the scabs off old wounds and confront what you fear most about yourself and the world. But you will also release a powerful, immutable force that exerts unseen, unknown and intangible energy. You will sing your songs with such creative force that you taste them in the back of your throat; you will write, paint, and dance with savage authenticity. The voice that emerges will be uniquely yours. It will lead you into the place where your essential truth dwells. It will be the voice of your blood, your soul, the part of you that pulls you down deep into your own being…where you belong.

*When it's over, I want to say: all my life
I was a bride married to amazement.*

—Mary Oliver

INTRODUCTION

Your spiritual self was born in a dream, and when you dream, you are returning home. Your natural self is at home in the land where everything is both a physical fact and a poetic metaphor. When you dream, you are returning to the home, the very womb of your spirit and a world that speaks the language of your soul.

— *Thomas Moore*

Daughter of Night

Before I opened up to my dream life, I was submerged in the messy interior of my monkey mind. I had an endless, internal grumble going on in my head. Like many contemporary women everywhere, I appeared clear-headed, cheerful, strong and independent. But secretly, I felt out of shape, self-conscious and self-loathing. As with other women, no one ever saw or suspected my secret life of discontent and sorrow. The voices inside my head were filled with a low, simmering annoyance, dissatisfaction and despair. I pined for a life of adventure and travel, but my determination to fulfill the roles of "Good Daughter" and "Good Wife" smothered and subdued me. I chose a subservient, homebound life and put my desire to go adventuring aside.

I bred dragons and devils in my heart, resenting the feelings that held me against my will. My spirit became displaced from its home within me. A constant monologue of vexation and exasperation took up residence within my mind. A song of sorrow became the soundtrack of my life, a refrain that endlessly repeated until it drowned out my connection to my soul. I aligned myself with a poverty of spirit as I took on an inner critic to keep me self-effacing and insecure. I allowed my self-esteem to degenerate.

Then, my dreams snared me with a host of chaotic images. My nights were filled with crimes committed, babies abandoned, bodies bruised, puppies drowned, and cars crushed. I was a fugitive from justice, unmasked and exposed. I was chased, arrested, wiped out and stuck in the mud. I lost my cell phone, my keys, my purse and my watch. I missed my flights, my classes and my appointments. I sank under quicksand. I fought with vandals and intruders.

I resisted opening this Pandora's box of dream images. But when I finally stopped pushing the difficult dreams away, my dream life began to germinate, and my outer life began to transform.

What is most alive of all is inside your own house.
—*Kabir*

Metamorphosis

As a small child, I loved visual art. But as I grew older, I could not replicate what I saw. And I believed that replication was the aim of art, so, like many children who hit this wall, I gave up all hope of becoming an artist. I grew up and went to college with this limiting belief firmly lodged in my consciousness. Having abandoned the visual arts, I found myself drawn to the study of literature. I became mesmerized by the many layers of symbolism embedded in twentieth-century English prose and poetry. I discovered how to uncover literary references in mythology, history, religion and the metaphysical arts. As I learned to read between the lines, I came to understand the power of language. I became a literary detective, plumbing the layers of metaphor and paradox in search of hidden meanings in modern fiction and verse.

But I was intimidated when it came to my own attempts at writing. I had no idea how to become a writer. What would I write about? I had some interesting dreams and thought I might turn them into poetry. I attempted a few poems and, eager for feedback, showed them to my English professor. He did not encourage me. He told me that dreams were a cop-out for writers and should not be taken seriously. Years later he regretted saying that, but the damage was done. I stopped writing and became convinced I would never be a writer.

As if my self-doubt was not enough, it was the prevailing notion in the mid-twentieth century that women could not be writers or artists. It was believed they had neither the talent nor temperament to succeed. If a woman insisted on trying to publish or exhibit artwork, she was advised to change her name to make it sound androgynous. Reinforced by these conventional beliefs, I remember thinking if I can't write like a man, then I am not going to write….if I can't paint like a man, I won't paint….

By the time I graduated from college, the women's liberation movement had taken over campuses everywhere. Antiquated notions of gender limitations in the arts were challenged and widely rejected. I was ostensibly liberated, yet I was still locked into feelings of inadequacy. After graduation, I had no plan for my life, so I jumped into my car and drove west to seek my fortune. I discovered Santa Fe, a town devoted to the arts. New Mexico's Native American, Spanish and contemporary craft traditions inspired me to immerse myself in weaving, spinning and dyeing. I became a designer of wearable art and founded the Santa Fe Weaving Gallery. But after many productive years as a craftswoman and business owner, I longed for my life to have a larger purpose; I was desperate to be a "real" artist, to make art that had significance and meaning. But how? I had no subject matter. I came up empty whenever I tried to find inspiration. I could not find a focus that called to me.

I knew that true art must come from within, so I began a practice of meditation in the form of active imagination. I experimented with Jungian and Shamanic journeys. I invented my own journeys. In a leap of faith, I walked away from my career to focus on my meditations as a way to connect with the source of a more creative life. I had just turned forty.

With my days free, I began my practice of active imagination in earnest. Every morning I embarked upon adventures in a vibrational universe filled with strange characters, animals and guides. I faithfully recorded and sketched my visions. These experiences never seemed like make-believe; they always felt real. I never thought I was just making stuff up. Yet there was still a pervasive sense of conscious control as I moved through my imaginal landscapes. I wanted to go beyond that control, but I didn't know how.

Then, one day, as I was deeply immersed in my meditation practice, a flyer appeared in my mailbox announcing that the International Association for the Study of Dreams (IASD) was to hold its tenth annual conference in Santa Fe. The topic of dreams still piqued my interest, as it had in college when I tried to turn dreams into poems. Over the years, I had written down a few dreams that intrigued me, but I didn't know how to understand them. I had acquired several books on dream interpretation but had never found them helpful. Still, the topic of dreaming seemed akin to the imaginative meditations I was already immersed in. An international conference on dreams in Santa Fe was a once-in-a-lifetime opportunity. So, I thought, "why not?" I sent in the registration fee.

The IASD conference lasted five days and altered my life forever. I explored my dreams in experiential workshop sessions led by prominent psychotherapists, educators, healers, shamans, writers and artists. I learned traditional and contemporary dreamwork techniques. I discovered the wealth of fascinating material that lay concealed in dreams. I became enchanted by their intelligence and mind-altering magic. The door to new worlds, mysterious and unexplored, suddenly opened before me. I saw how attending to my dreams could cultivate the creative authenticity I sought.

Before long, my curiosity was fully engaged in deciphering my dreams. I filled my journal with observations, ruminations, sketches and scribblings. My creative life unfolded, revealing layers and facets of rich nuance, meaning and grace. I recovered a sense of self that would have otherwise been lost. As a result of working with my dreams, I found the source of my creativity. I reinvented my life. I invented uncommon and unorthodox methods for accessing dreams. I taught workshops across the USA and abroad. And now, many decades after embarking on this soulful journey, I have written this book to share my approach to creative forms of dreamwork with fellow seekers who have restless minds, wandering souls and tender hearts.

The pandemic of 2020 put a sudden stop to my globetrotting days. Nevertheless, I had access to a multiverse of adventures and escapades in the imaginal world of dreams. I swam underwater while breathing. I levitated, I floated, I flew. I sang old show tunes with six baby alligators and danced with wild birds in cowboy boots. I watched a lion swallow a tiger. I took cooking lessons from Picasso. I had lunch with Joseph of Arimathea. My ex-husband became engaged to Hagrid. I met up with Elvis, Debbie Reynolds, Ram Das, a dying friend, three former lovers and a Jungian scholar. I strangled a little dictator. I gave an elephant a pedicure, I wore a big yellow chicken outfit to a wedding, I dressed like a counterfeit woman, I visited with dead people, I pushed the nuclear button, I was a big woman with a big dream….

And I completed this book.

The spirit of the depths took my understanding and all my knowledge and placed them at the service of the inexplicable and the paradoxical.
—C.G. Jung

*We all begin the process before we are ready,
before we are strong enough,
before we know enough;*

*We begin a dialogue with thoughts and feelings
that both tickle and thunder within us.*

*We respond before we know how to speak the language,
before we know all the answers,
and before we know exactly to whom we are speaking.*
—Clarissa Pinkola Estés

INVITATION

Wherever you are is the entry point.

—*Kabir*

A DreamingArts Adventure

I invite you to share in a most extraordinary adventure. It's an inner journey—to the wild and enigmatic landscape of dreams. In this book, you will find numerous activities to choose from that will stimulate your creativity. The dreamwork practice I call DreamingArts is unlike other conventional dreamwork you may be familiar with. As you engage with the DreamingArts activities and processes in Conversations with Psyche, you will undoubtedly find yourself in uncharted waters. Like deep-sea diving, the DreamingArts can take you from the consensual world of your waking hours and plunge you into a universe that teems with enchantment and surprise. This practice can send you on an inter-dimensional voyage into a mysterious domain, where enigmatic ambiguities, quirky pranks, and profoundly paradoxical tales present themselves regularly. As you learn to navigate this realm, you will tap into the immense wisdom and creative power your nighttime visions hold. The projects and activities within the pages of this book will inspire and guide your exploration into the hidden contours of your heart and soul.

The Conversation

Like a tired wanderer who had sought nothing in the world apart from her, shall I come closer to my soul. I shall learn that my soul finally lies behind everything, and if I cross the world, I am ultimately doing this to find my soul.
—C.G. Jung

This book is titled *Conversations with Psyche* because dreams offer us a chance to have in-depth, ongoing conversations with our souls. In Greek mythology, Psyche was a beautiful, mortal princess who fell in love with the divine god of love, Eros. Before she was allowed to marry him, the princess had to endure harrowing trials, culminating with a journey to the underworld. This is why Psyche is the warrior/shepherdess of souls who can lead us on our nocturnal ramblings.

As the guardian of dreams and siren of the night, Psyche wears a cloak of darkness and walks in the shadows, calling up our visions. She is a soothsayer, a sage and a shapeshifter, a bender of space and a folder of time. She is an emissary of wisdom and an agent of truths, a holy sorceress who stirs our emotions and plunges us into her dark, alchemistic brew: one part chaos, one part wisdom. Psyche is a teacher and an oracle who trades in secret codes and symbols. Mercurial and unpredictable, she is a conjurer, a provocateur, a stirrer of pots and a spinner of worlds. She is the ultimate high-wire artist: unafraid and unflinching. She is a master storyteller, a dramatist, a mystery writer and an absurdist. She can be a trickster and a taunt, a tease who can be equally lurid and loving. She dispatches angels and demons alike and casts shadows, both dark and bright. She can terrify, confuse, soothe and inspire—sometimes all at once.

Psyche does not bother to be subtle or polite, nor is she interested in exercising censorship, caution or restraint. For her, no subject matter is off-limits or out of bounds. She cares not for your comfort or pride—only for the welfare of your soul. Once summoned, Psyche will come. She will stand over your shoulder, guiding you on odysseys of discovery, the dimensions you can barely imagine when you first start out.

Be forewarned, though: if you respond to Psyche's call, there will be consequences. She is the mistress of Duende; she pushes and prods, sometimes uncomfortably so. She will kick you out of the nest of your familiarity, complacency and security. You will sail to the edge of your known world and be asked to go beyond. She will expose your weaknesses, foibles and vanities in all their disguises. You will be confronted with aspects of yourself that you tend to hide, repress or deny. You will open your heart and expose yourself to all the saints and sinners within. You will engage with your fears and dance with your devils. You will be chased by beasts of your own making and be asked to grapple with your monsters. Psyche will test you; she will test your resolve, your fortitude and your commitment. She will teach you lessons you didn't know you needed to learn. She will take you, dream by dream, into the heart of the labyrinth of your mind and heart.

This work takes tenacity and courage. The journey is arduous and, like Psyche's, can be harrowing. Undertake this quest only if you are willing to venture beyond your comfort level and confound your center of gravity.

But rest assured, Psyche will also acknowledge your gifts, your talents and the most luminous aspects of your being. She will lift you up with a glowing portrait of your inner beauty and wisdom. She will help you to heal your relationships with your family, your community, your world and your soul-self. She will guide you to see the mythic dimensions of your life and show you that your stories are vastly more significant than you ever thought. She will prove to you that you are a vital part of the fabric of the universe and that you matter.

A dream can be the highest point of a life.
—Ben Okri

The DreamingArts

The DreamingArts practice, as explored in this book, will introduce you to Psyche and invite you to start a conversation with her. You will find creative activities that combine insights and skills to guide you through multi-level interpretations that weave together depth psychology, mysticism, mythology, science and spirituality in engaging pathways that combine writing craft, artistry and a touch of wizardry. You can use these approaches as stepping stones to lead you through the unfamiliar terrain of your unconscious while enhancing your introspective thinking, art-making and verbal expression. They can also provide a structure to form a dream group or inspire an established group. (See the section titled "Guidelines for Dream Groups.")

Through dream journal entries, morning pages and prompts, you will develop the ability to expand the narrative of your dream stories. When you earnestly listen to your dreams, tend them like a garden and probe them for their secrets, they will reveal a wellspring of powerful images and ideas. The more you write about your dreams, the more your dreams will provide you with fresh material. Writer's/Artist's block will no longer exist.

In waking life, emotions may often feel too raw to confront openly, but the symbolic language of dreams provides a protected place to rant and rave in a secret code. As you peer through the mask of metaphoric language and mythic images, you will begin to recognize and safely decipher what you have found. The DreamingArts process invites you to express yourself with a wild voice that quivers with excitement and whispers with vulnerability.

Before long, something magical will happen: you will locate the source of your creativity. With perseverance, you will establish a stronger connection to your dreams and gain a firm grasp of your interpretive skills. Your voice will pour forth as you describe otherworldly visions, potent emotions and vivid memories. Your images will blossom with fully expressed honesty and passion. You will compose compelling, visionary stories and create new worlds with ink. The paintings you paint and the collage pictures you find will spring from your hands. Music played, sung and danced will flow. Your inner world will grow, expand and deepen.

Truth is One. Paths are Many.
—*Sri Swami Satchidananda*

A Mind of Your Own

You can find a profusion of books with different approaches to uncovering the meaning of dreams. Many focus on the therapeutic aspects of dreams, notably in classics by the great forefathers of modern psychology. Indigenous and spiritual dream books focus on the mystical elements of dreams. Some books delve into scientific research regarding the physical mechanics of how we dream. Some books examine the mind-expanding field of lucid dreaming. There are beautifully illustrated coffee-table books on dreams, books that tell fortunes and a plethora of dream symbol dictionaries that offer countless interpretations.

My focus here is to look at the world of dreams from outside analytical, scientific, clinical and oracular perspectives. This book is filled with guidance, creativity tools and journal techniques that will introduce you to the language of dreams, so you won't need to search outside yourself for translation or analysis. This is a book of possibilities, not of directions or interpretations. Whether you read it, cover to cover, or just dip in and out, the DreamingArts practice will lead you down a path of discovery toward unexpected surprises and insightful "Aha" moments.

You can do this! You do not have to have a Ph.D. in Depth Psychology or follow any religious faith, spiritual practice or belief system. No matter what you see as your limits or constraints in waking life, your dreaming mind knows no such bounds. All you need is a dream and the curiosity to explore it. Almost everyone remembers at least one dream, which is enough to start. You do not need to be a frequent flier—but you do need to be willing to soar. Just know that it may take some time and effort to hear the subtleties of what your dream world has to say.

The magnitude of potential explanations and interpretations for dreams and their symbols can seem overwhelmingly impossible to grasp. It is tempting to want to turn to dream symbol books to find out what the "experts" have to say. But there is no one dream symbol dictionary or online site that can speak to the unique complexity that is you. Symbol dictionaries deal with dream images generally, not personally, and can be confusing and misleading. They address concepts, not feelings. They tend to focus on a single psychoanalytic, religious, mythic or superstitious source and can overwhelm you with contradictory beliefs, fortune-cookie predictions or misleading cultural assumptions.

No single dream dictionary can give a broad range of interpretations relevant and specific to your dream. If you attempt to "analyze" a dream, searching for a singular explanation, you close yourself to dream inquiry's poetic and creative possibilities. It's advisable to resist the urge to evaluate your dreams with symbol books before you open your dreams in more introspective ways. The act of "interpreting" requires a rational mindset, whereas the DreamingArts initiative offers a more flexible approach that enables you to bypass the cognitive part of your mind.

But, if you do look in dream symbol books and websites, do not rely on any one source. Inquiry into the literal meanings and metaphoric associations of dream images can seed and feed the imagination and stoke the creative fires. The best dream symbol tools are an ordinary dictionary, a thesaurus and an encyclopedia. Word definitions, etymology, synonyms and idioms reveal thought-provoking insights through unexpected wordplay and expressive language. Encyclopedic sources can be used to research literary, historical and biographical references and proffer significant cultural observations. Mythological and metaphysical reference works can acquaint you with the influence of archetypes and ancient philosophies. It is well worth delving into time-honored reference books, but I encourage you to do your own groundwork first, think for yourself and trust the DreamingArts process.

As you explore the DreamingArts activities, the enigmatic terrain of your soul will become terra cognita. In that newly known land, you will navigate the intricacies of the dreamscape with expanded skills of imagination. When you delve into your dreams and write about them from your inner, most authentic self, you will be richly rewarded. The journey will ask a lot of you in return; what you get from it depends on your willingness to engage. This is contemplative work but needs to be entered into in the spirit of play. Playfulness can loosen the shackles of the intellect as creative forms of dreamwork become your key to an infinite, imaginal universe.

Psyche thrives in a committed relationship and enjoys your active engagement. Your inner life will change when you listen to her song as it blows like a mistral wind through your psychic landscape. Your DreamingArts practice will lead you to experience breathtaking and revelatory moments of allegory, paradox, metaphor and mythological symbols and archetypes. You will discover a gossamer thread leading you through the labyrinth of your dreamscapes. When you take hold of it in one hand and your pen in the other, you will embark on an endless, ever-unfolding soul journey with a new appreciation for the depths of your own being. Your creativity will pour forth, and life itself will become fuller.

*Nourishing your imaginal life through dreamwork
is an exquisite way to feed your soul.*
—Bambi Corso-Steinmeyer

Dreams are the most curious asides and soliloquies of the soul. When a man recollects his dream, it is like meeting the ghost of himself. Dreams often surprise us into the strangest self-knowledge.

—*Alexander Smith*

PART I
ABOUT DREAMS

A Separate Reality

Dreams are often most profound when they seem the most crazy.
—Sigmund Freud

Once tucked in your bed and the inky darkness thickens around you, you nod off. Soon you surrender to a mysterious process no one fully understands; a meandering river of images flows through you—multi-dimensional, kaleidoscopic and mysterious. The river fills with a multitude of fantastical lifeforms from unfamiliar regions of the mind. This nocturnal river is a mirror of your soul where you can dive into the truth of who you are.

But dreams are transient visitors, prone more to slip through your fingers than to linger. They are mercurial, ethereal, intangible. When you catch one, it can slither out of your conscious awareness and back into the depths, where it can disintegrate or fade away without a trace. When dreams allow themselves to be caught, they tend to arrive as a mystery that the pragmatic mind cannot easily decode. They come from an aspect of the mind different from everyday consciousness. They exist in another realm—the realm of the imagination. They emerge unbidden in a pastiche of conundrums and bizarre juxtapositions. They are filled with implausible actions, physical anomalies, and perverse incongruities, where the laws of nature are ignored or repealed. What we know as reality is inverted in a parallel universe that operates by vastly different rules from those of the physical world.

Dreams come as a jumble of images in a crazy quilt of impressions often strung together in a sequence that bears little resemblance to waking logic. They fracture time. Scenes from memories may be sutured together out of sequence. Past, present, and future co-exist in a perpetual landscape of possibility. Things happen in dreamtime that otherwise could not.

Dream visions, voices and events reveal a strange and inscrutable world. Dream beings shatter old paradigms and gleefully poke fingers at our sanctimonious beliefs and inflated pretensions. Tricksters populate our dreams as jokers, clowns, pranksters, beggars, rule-breakers and wise fools. Dream archetypes appear both light and dark, heroic and villainous, foolish and wise, benign and malicious. Dream themes break taboos, revel in the destruction of the known, and shatter old ideologies.

Dreams seem alien, mysterious and unfathomable to those steeped in rationality. Dreams use cryptic, symbolic language filled with puzzling paradoxes, contradictions, indirect references and riddles with no rational answers or meanings. We must learn to shift away from our usual reasoning strategies to make sense of them. Dreams are simply not of waking reality. The only ways to engage with them are ways that do not try to oversimplify, confine, define or rationalize them.

A dream is not a singular entity with just one identity or message. There are many pathways to the interior land of the soul. Dreams are polysensical, with layers of substance and significance. The layers intermingle to create an infinitely rich ecosystem, a complex, interconnected web of possibilities in which the structure of your whole being is interwoven. The meaning of a dream is not fixed, and it is never final; it evolves with your engagement.

The tools and practices you will learn in this book will guide you in letting go of who you think you are and what you already know about yourself. DreamingArts activities offer a variety of techniques for exploring the mysteries and magic of the dream world. All that is required of you is to disengage from your pragmatic, logical left brain and allow yourself to experiment freely with your intuitive right brain about irrational, illogical and seemingly impossible things.

To start this practice, simply go to sleep!

Big Dreams, Little Dreams

Dreams are like hundreds of forms all pointing to the inner center.
—*Marie-Louise von Franz*

Some dreams are unmistakable Big Dreams—saber-rattling, technicolor, mythic, transcendent. Throughout the histories of indigenous and biblical cultures, the dreams in sacred texts and teachings have been regarded as communications from the spiritual realm. Visionary and divine nocturnal experiences occur to most people at least once in a lifetime. Whether we are spiritual, religious, agnostic or atheistic doesn't matter. Big Dreams connect us to the immensity of spirit through awe-inspiring glimpses of a mystical dimension, a visitation from otherworldly beings, an expansion of sensation or an alternative awareness of space and time.

Big Dreams are the ones we tend to remember all our lives. But no dream is truly small. No matter how trivial or insignificant it might appear at a first waking glance, try not to dismiss any dream. Even the most mundane dream story can reveal hidden jewels of insight. So, don't be fooled. Unpretentious dream characters may appear too minor to attract your attention; inconsequential dream objects may be taken for granted. Dream actions may seem insignificant, and dream sensations may seem negligible. Yet, every image in a dream can be meaningful and evocative.

Often, dreams are characterized by missing links between scenes, figures without faces, voices without bodies and rooms without windows or doors. Someone or something you expected to be present may not actually be there. What (or who) is missing in your dream is often just as important as what (or who) is present.

Each dream is uniquely tailored to your individual nature, physical and emotional state, environment, childhood background, family dynamic, career path, aspirations, political views and spiritual beliefs. Moreover, your dreaming mind contains the genesis of human consciousness, where universal primal patterns of existence unveil essential truths underlying all humanity. Your dreams manifest themselves in diverse ways, ranging from the "little dreams" with personal details of your daily life to the "big dreams" that connect you to the fundamental truths and mysteries of the collective unconscious.

Across the Great Divide

"Who are you?" Asks the Caterpillar. "I hardly know." Replies Alice.

—*Lewis Carroll*

A third of our time on earth is spent sleeping, and about one-quarter of that time is spent dreaming. Yet our dreams—if we remember them at all—are too frequently regarded as nothing more than odd little anecdotes. We tend to write them off as misfiring synapses, explain them away as a jumble of day residue or simply disregard them altogether. In doing so, we miss the limitless supply of extraordinary narratives that play inside us every night.

Without the tools to nurture our psychic reveries, most of us habitually look to external sources for inspiration and revelation. We immerse ourselves in other people's stories and inventions. We read books, attend performances, watch films and stream video clips. We surf the internet, yearning to stimulate the imaginative creativity we feel is missing from our lives. But everything we need—and more—lies within us.

According to current research being done in the field of neuroscience, our conscious mind makes up only ten percent of our mind's capacity while a vast reservoir of knowing lies below the surface in the unconscious. Our dreams contain a connection to this vast source. Dreams are our motherlodes of boundless ingenuity, invention and creativity.

Inner City

Encountering all these strange creatures & events seems to fill my head with ideas, says Alice, only I don't exactly know what they are!
—*Lewis Carroll*

With few exceptions, all sentient beings dream. Typically, nearly all humans (unless severely traumatized) dream close to every ninety minutes throughout the night. Most dreams occur during the stage of sleep called REM (Rapid Eye Movement), the rapid movement of the eyes being a distinguishing characteristic of the dream stage of sleep. In the beginning of the night, REM cycles are short, occurring as the body catches up on physical rest, but they increase in length throughout the night. The more time we sleep, the more chance we have for longer, extended and more memorable dreams.

Research has shown that our brains are very active during REM sleep. Recent neurological findings have revealed that dreams are created from a complex brain circuit of cognition distinct from reasoning, conscious, waking thoughts. The active brain areas in the REM state involve separate neural pathways for adaptive learning and creative insight. As a result, dreams help us resolve problems, process emotions and integrate memories.

Scientists know that dreams are essential for our physical and emotional health and that dream deprivation causes difficulty concentrating and a tendency toward hallucinations. Studies show that subjects deprived of dreams, experience increased tension, anxiety and depression, as well as weight gain and lack of coordination.

Yet, although the function of dreaming has been studied with rigorous scientific methodology, the meaning of dreams is still not fully understood. Dreams pose a problem for Western science-oriented minds. Because the night mind is littered with absurdity, irrationality and contradiction, many scientists give little credence to the meaning of dream content. Science has a low tolerance for ambiguity, and dreams simply do not fit into any system of rational logic. They are unique, ephemeral experiences with no measurable depth, density or opacity. Dreams cannot be recorded, photographed or projected on a screen for scrutiny. They are not quantifiable. For all these reasons, science does not fully understand how the dreaming mind works.

A prime reason for this paucity of dream findings is that Newtonian physics still forms the basis of much of modern science. From this perspective, everything is thought to have just one nature. Things are what they are; their meaning is fixed. Everything studied can be neatly categorized. This supposition rests on a theory known as "scientific materialism": matter is what matters. In this worldview, the universe is akin to a clockwork, a perfect machine separate from us. Thus, observing and studying the world from a removed and objective stance is the accepted scientific procedure. Everything, including consciousness, results from some kind of material interaction of chemical and electrical interface occurring in the brain.

The new physics, however, challenges the notion that our world is composed of discrete, separate things. Contemporary science now asserts that we exist in a participatory universe. In the Quantum view, the universe does not exist "out there," detached from us. Instead, everything exists in relationship with everything else. The universe is not fixed or static; it is animate, alive and continuously moving, constantly changing and evolving. And because everything is interconnected, our thoughts and actions, no matter how small or insignificant they may seem, affect what the universe becomes. In other words, we are all in relationship with the universe. Whether we realize it consciously or not, we are constantly communicating with it, and it is communicating with us. Ironically, recent experiments in physics have verified and rejuvenated an ancient worldview long held by indigenous shamanic cultures: everything is connected. Therefore, it stands to reason that dreams are a part of this universal amalgamation.

Down-to-earth, no-nonsense, matter-of-fact individuals may view dreams skeptically yet, revered writers, artists, poets, musicians and filmmakers—even Nobel Laureate scientists and inventors—have always known that dreams influence creative inspiration. Great geniuses from Einstein to Niels Bohr, Benjamin Franklin to Descartes, Beethoven to Bach, Mondrian to Dali, Bram Stoker to H.G. Wells, Paul McCartney to Keith Richards, have produced groundbreaking inventions like the theory of relativity, the structure of the atom, the double helix structure of DNA, Google, the sewing machine and the ballpoint pen, as well as great works of art like the Messiah, Wild Strawberries, 8 ½, Jane Eyre, Frankenstein, Dr. Jekyll and Mr Hyde, Rite of Spring, Satisfaction, Terminator, and Sophie's Choice.

Fear of Freud

We can't stay attached to old ideas and old ways of seeing the world and achieve illumination. By definition, to have a new vision is to make a willing sacrifice of some old way of thinking and seeing.

—David Gordon

Sigmund Freud, the founder of psychoanalysis, declared that dreams are the "Royal Road" to the unconscious. In his famous book *The Interpretation of Dreams*, Freud stresses that dreams should be interpreted as evidence of wish fulfillment, particularly emphasizing that many symbols in dreams, notably those resembling genitalia—skyscrapers or caverns, rockets or pockets—represent something sexual. His theory has haunted Western culture ever since. Many people still live under Freud's far-reaching influence feeling shamed and embarrassed by dreams, connecting them with wicked desires, especially when graphic, bawdy or perverse. As a culture, we have been victimized by the frightening prospect that if we share our dreams, others will know our deepest, darkest, most private thoughts. We avoid talking about our dreams, fearing they might reveal disgraceful, repressed yearnings buried below our awareness.

Nowadays, many modern methods of dreamwork challenge Freud's assumptions. We are now encouraged to think beyond the unsettling analysis of what we might consider scurrilous and scandalous. The libido, once associated solely with sexual desires, is today commonly considered a healthy expression of our life force, our vital energy. Rather than concluding that bizarre dreams mean we are psychologically depraved, today's depth psychologists ask us to consider that every dream offers a range of possible relevant interpretations. Carl Jung called dreams "a little hidden door in the innermost and most secret recesses of the psyche" without adjudging dreams as exclusive expressions of libido. He explained dreams as an inner map of an individual's evolution toward a more balanced relationship between the ego and the unconscious. Numerous forms of contemporary dreamwork now follow the fundamentals of Jung's approach to dreams as the study of the most intimate sanctum of the soul.

Inhabiting Your Dreams

If you don't know where you are going, any road will get you there.
(Cheshire Cat) Lewis Carroll

There is no one correct way to open up a dream, but a good strategy in creative dreamwork is to start with an open mind. Dreams do not come to tell you what you already know. Looking only at the surface appearance, you might think you understand a dream, but an initial impression only reveals a small portion of the numerous messages it may contain. There is so much more to your night visions than you may first notice. Dreams always hold some surprises!

 The path forward is seldom direct or linear. The DreamingArts activities foster spiralic thinking, by which you can meander in and around your dream territory, getting impressions and noticing sparks of recognition and insight. "Spiralic thinking" is organic and evolutionary. It engages you through free association in ever-expanding circles of connection. It does not proceed like an arrow but rather like a convoluted coil that lifts you to many levels of self-awareness. This process connects one insight to another in a continuous, widening helix. By staying in a state of curiosity and wonderment, you will find answers to questions you didn't even know you were asking.

The Poetics of Paradox

Our life is an apprenticeship to the truth that around every circle another can be drawn; … under every deep a lower deep opens.
—*Ralph Waldo Emerson*

The practice of the DreamingArts is indirect and right-brained. As such, it will never be precise or regimented. You don't have to think linearly or logically. The malleability of grammar and vocabulary in dreamspeak is playful and slippery. The language used to record dream images can mean one thing and also its opposite. You may notice yourself employing peculiar modes of expression, invented words and antiquated phrases.
Your syntax and grammatical blunders may seem scrambled to your rational mind, but accidental misspellings and odd word choices can function like encryption keys. Double entendre, idiomatic expressions, jargon and puns can unlock new arenas of surprising innuendo and meaning.

Lost and Found

We know all too well that few journeys are linear & predictable. Instead, they swerve & turn, twist & double back, until we don't know if we're coming or going.
—Phil Cousineau

To explore a dream through the DreamingArts practice is to set off on a journey without instruments or maps, letting the night winds and other influences take you where they will. At the beginning of the journey, your trail will zigzag this way and that, twisting all about, without rhyme and most certainly without reason. You may be blessed with a quick insight or moment of clarity, or the trail might disappear entirely. You must be willing to lose your bearings, surrender to not-knowing, leave the known world behind and step into uncharted territories without a clear destination. When you feel most lost, when the ego is defeated, and your guard is down—that is when you will be able to traverse forms of consciousness beyond the limitations of time and space.

Time Out of Mind

We are somewhat more than ourselves in our sleep;
the slumber of the body seems to be the waking of the soul.
—*Sir Thomas Browne*

The practice of DreamingArts is a way of knowing without thinking. Psyche will help you; she is a soul guide adept at leading seekers through transformative experiences. She is a mediator between the conscious and the unconscious realms. She serves as a psychopomp, traversing between the plane of consensus reality and the spirit world, bringing back energy, knowledge and wisdom. As you learn to understand her language of dreams, she will visit you in many forms. She will help you to straddle the liminal space between worlds where you will be able to connect your waking, conscious awareness to your deeper unconscious dreaming mind. You will become the intermediary between these worlds, the shaman of your own transformational process.

Sleeping with the Enemy

No matter what form the dragon may take, it is the mysterious passage past him, or into his jaws, that stories of any depth will be concerned to tell.
—Flannery O'Connor

The DreamingArts are not a panacea, remedy or instant antidote to a lifetime of challenges and wounds. It takes time to unwind the ties that bind us. Dreams often show us aspects of ourselves we may have rejected, repressed or disowned. The emotions that accompany such dreams can be overpowering. Giving credence to shadowy dream images is a struggle for many of us. We tend to be seekers of light, and dreams' dark content may seem antithetical to our beliefs. Dream beings are often amoral, perverse or cruel. They come in the guise of apocryphal villains and grotesque creatures who speak blasphemy and act irreverently. The content of disturbing dreams can be painful and embarrassing. But if we deny the parts of ourselves that we don't want to acknowledge, hidden layers of protection become more complex with time. When we avoid the dark shadows in our dreams, some of the best parts of ourselves get hidden away as well.

Knowledge of the shadow is essential to a creative's toolbox. The DreamingArts uses discomfort as fuel for juicy writing and art-making. An artist cannot paint anything of merit by rendering only light; there is no poetry, literature or drama without conflict, emotion and complex characters. Even if you feel initially afraid or repelled by your dreams, the DreamingArts invite you to explore scary themes with an imaginative response. When uncomfortable feelings arise, leap into your barrel of piranhas, hurl yourself into the abyss, cry out, keen and rage. Look deep into the eyes of your monsters, for they are part of who you are.

If ever you have the rare opportunity to speak with the devil, then do not forget to confront him in all seriousness. He is your devil, after all.
—C.G. Jung

Recurring Dreams

The journey always begins with the calling. The old system of doing things, the rules, the strategies that once were successful on a personal, professional, or societal level are no longer effective. Our dreams are calling us to change or grow. We can resist the calling, but it will come again and again.

—David Gordon, Ph.D.

We often find ourselves on a journey that leads full circle back to all we thought we left behind. Our nocturnal narratives whirl about like revolving gears in a relentlessly moving machine. We circumnavigate around an orbit of adventures where we spiral in and out of repeating themes. We find ourselves striving and struggling with unresolved redundancy. Recurring images haunt us. Familiar figures chase us with relics of unfinished business or unresolved issues.

A recurring dream is one of the tricks Psyche uses to get you to pay attention. She knows how distracted and inattentive you can be, so she uses repetitive dreams to send a message you have ignored or refused to acknowledge. The cumulative impact of these repetitive dreams can make you feel trapped, controlled and unable to change the channel. You may feel stuck in a rotating carousel of thoughts and feelings.

However, if you practice recording your recurring dreams, you will notice that you rarely have the exact same dream. Most often, some detail changes. Two-bit, small-fry, low-ranking fragments are often overshadowed, overlooked and ignored. Obscure references may slip by practically unnoticed. Archiving your dreams will help to capture minor details. These small artifacts hold clues that can tell you how the dream's meaning is shifting over time. Seemingly irrelevant elements can contain significant insights. Every detail matters.

Nightmares and Disturbing Dreams

You've got to be willing to boogie with the boogie man.

—*Gregg Levoy*

Dreams rarely float lightly on pink ponies over cotton candy clouds; they are often seeded with dark matter. Dreams are filled with bullies and tyrants, chaos and catastrophes. These difficult dreams appear when our old systems break down, when the rules and the strategies no longer serve us. Often, what we will remember most about a dream is the acute emotional impact left in its wake. Dreams can take us to the edge of our fears. We may burst awake from circumstances we can't control, feeling rattled, shattered, torn asunder. Nothing has happened in waking life, yet we are unnerved, our hearts scorched and pounding, our blood curdled. Dreams can leave us wallowing in a pool of anxiety or overcome by the shame of unwanted feelings.

    These difficult dreams bring us face to face with our vulnerabilities, our deepest sorrows, our guilts and our fears. A nightmare can stir us to the core, disrupt our innermost composure and cut right through to our soul. The reality of the dream world can hold us in its imaginal grip at the point of a knife.

    As a tender of dreams, your challenge is to meet your bêtes noires in their contradictory lawlessness without judgment, retreat or recoil. Do not believe the voices that say you are not strong or brave or courageous enough, for that is the fear speaking.

    The DreamingArts practice can develop your inner strength and resilience, whereby you can refuse the tyranny of nightmares and alter repetitive dreams. Like a gardener, you have to dig in the dirt if you want creativity to thrive. Nightmares are a fertile ground where tremendous growth and expansion occur. To reach your center, you must be willing to encounter the monsters within. Once confronted, a nightmare cannot hold its power over you.

Wounded Healer

To be wounded means also to have the Healing Power activated in us...maybe the very purpose of the wound is to make us aware of the healing power in us.
—*Alfred Adler*

In homeopathy, poisons like arsenic, mercury, snake venom and belladonna are distilled into medicines. That which causes the disease can help to heal it. Similarly, creative dreamwork can help mend wounds by distilling adversity and heartache into small doses. Touching the wound through the DreamingArts can be a significant step in the journey from woundedness into wholeness. The cure comes from finding a meaning to painful dreams.

Handle with Care

If we don't metabolize what has happened, we might metastasize it.
—Linda Yael Schiller

The DreamingArts offer a balance where suffering and joy can coexist. When you use creative techniques to address the darkness in your dreams, repressed psychic forces can balance themselves and restore a sense of equilibrium. Facing difficult dreams through the arts is an established psychotherapeutic protocol for reducing nightmare potency and frequency. But since nightmares link up with anger, heartbreak and trauma, it is beneficial to approach these dreams in the company of a therapist or a dream group, who can support you and encourage you to see beyond the literal dream story into healing metaphors. (See Appendix B: DreamingArts as a Therapeutic Tool for Psychotherapy).

Impossible Odds

You were wild once. Don't let them tame you.
—Isadora Duncan

You do not have to remain stuck with a disturbing or unresolved dream. You can employ the DreamingArts to loosen the tenacity of fearful or frightening visions. You have permission from established psychoanalytic protocols to confront your dreams and to change the outcomes. You can harness your creative powers to take unconventional leaps forward, change your narratives and invent new outcomes. The DreamingArts will help you confront your villains, conquer impossible odds, triumph over conflicts and escape the inescapable.

A Dreamer's Declaration of Independence

(Adapted from the United States Declaration of Independence)

*Whenever any dream becomes destructive,
it is the right of the dreamer to alter it
and to institute a new dream....*

*Prudence must dictate that long-established recurring dream themes
should not be changed for light causes or frivolous whims.*

*However, we are more disposed to suffer than to abolish the forms
to which we have become accustomed.*

*So, when dreams of abuse or torment come,
and we feel reduced by their absolute despotism,
it is our right to throw off the tyranny of such dreamings,
and to provide new models for our future health and well-being.*

My Process, My Practice

At the end of the day, when the sun falls a willing prisoner of the night...and I become submitted to the mistress of the dark...the psyche expresses freely what my subconscious is afraid to give free rein. And there and then, between the play of reality and dreamland, I find my place. I find myself.

—*Eiry Nieves*

When I first awaken, I am between worlds. While I still have access to the realm of dreams, I try not to get up too quickly or abruptly. In this dreamy, half-awake state, before the dreams scatter, I jot down everything I can recall, no matter how small the fragment, without judging whether the dream has anything meaningful to impart. After jotting down my quick, initial waking notes, I get up, make a cup of tea and grab my laptop. Then I sit back down with my scribbled notes and copy them into a text document. My initial dream notes are sketchy and incomplete, so I fill in details I can remember.

I typically type my dream narrative as a free-verse prose poem. I don't worry about rhyme, word choices or rules of poetry; I simply restructure the sentences, letting the words fall into casual phrasings. When I shorten the lines, the isolation of images and actions invariably unveils hints about some of the dream's emotionally tender spots.

Once I have filled in as much detail as I can recall, I record the date. I devise a title that encapsulates the essence of the dream. Next, I write notes in my Life Log about whatever I was doing or thinking during the day(s) before I had the dream. When I record associations, memories and emotions that are triggered, valuable insights and epiphanies often come to the surface.

When pressed for time, I may stop my morning practice to carry out the day's obligations, appointments and tasks. But when time permits, I open up my dreams using one or more DreamingArts activities in the following chapters. I begin by deconstructing the elements of which my dream is composed. I list the dream people, animals, inanimate objects, settings, actions and emotions. I jot down a few definitions and descriptions as I make the list. I look for wordplays and puns. I delve into my memories. I search dictionaries to clarify key words and the thesaurus for synonyms. I Google literary, historical, mythological and archetypal references to expand my knowledge of the dream images that have caught my curiosity. I toggle back and forth online and in source books, spelunking for intriguing definitions and expressive vocabulary. When confusion arises (as it always does), I riff and sketch aimlessly, attuning to the eccentricities of Psyche's mysterious missives.

Each week, I choose one dream to work on in-depth in my DreamingArts Studio Workshops. The studio is a full-immersion creative cocoon far from ordinary time and space where DreamingArts projects invariably lead to breakthroughs, turning points, realizations and revelations. Alongside my students, I write poetry, illustrate hand-made dream books or make sets of collage dream cards.

….And you O my soul where you stand,
Surrounded, detached, in measureless oceans of space,
Ceaselessly musing, venturing, throwing, seeking the spheres to connect them,
Till the bridge you will need be form'd, till the ductile anchor hold,
Till the gossamer thread you fling catch somewhere, O my soul.
—Walt Whitman

PART II

THE MUSE IN THE NIGHT

The Encounter: The Conversation Dreams

My soul answered,
"Do you still not know that you are not writing a book to feed your vanity, but that you are speaking with me?"

—C. G. Jung

For years, the notion of writing "Conversations with Psyche" called to me. I had my heart set on sharing The DreamingArts as a pathway to the source of soulful creativity. I yearned to tie a ribbon around my signature work in the field of dreams. I longed to carve out my legacy. But organizing years of material and writing a formal book overwhelmed me. I felt consumed by my hunger for a wider audience yet strangled by insecurity and a crushing lack of confidence, which resulted in crippling self-censure. I went through spurts of unwavering focused energy followed by long periods of inertia. I spiraled upward with the euphoric trajectory of manic writing sprints, only to have my momentum dashed to the ground from neglect and stagnation.

My dreams mirrored my struggle. They called to me and challenged me to write this book while they mocked me by belittling my aspirations and criticizing my abilities. My dreams echoed my twisted perception that I was not good enough, smart enough or educated enough to write a book. I dreamt that misfits were navigating my ship, my flying potato was too heavy to get off the ground, a rat was gnawing mercilessly on my neck. And yet, simultaneously, my dreams were consecrated by the guidance of angels with open arms, gurus walking beside me, ornate butterflies in my attic and flowers blooming in the dark.

The dreams made it clear that I could wallow in despair or embrace the fire in my belly. They exposed the vanity that could drag me down, the insecurity that could defeat me or the higher purpose that could elevate my writing. I came to befriend my internal monsters, provocative tricksters and spiritual guides. I was shown that this work was not an act of hubris but a calling to enrich the creative lives of fellow dreamers. My dreams assured me that I was meant to write this book…. And that my life's work in dreams was worthwhile.

In this chapter, I use a selection of my dreams and contemplations to illustrate how dreams have companioned me through the writing of this book. They illustrate how the metaphoric language of dreams gave birth to my voice as a writer. Despite each dream having many layers and meanings, I have chosen to focus on one thematic thread to illustrate my challenges in bringing this book into being. I've selected a series of short dreams with which I hope you will feel some rapport. I present them as short free verse poems and follow them with contemplations, ruminations and riffs taken from my dream journal. Although this series of dreams point to the singularity of my own struggles as a writer, they also touch on the highs and lows we all experience when engaged in the creative process. I share my dreams in the hopes that you see parallels to your own journey and that they inspire you to use your dreams to fulfill your unique creative endeavors.

The Blind Boatman

An odd little boat
Sailing over high waves.
It has come to pick me up.
I am excited but apprehensive.
The water is choppy.
The little boat will get tossed around on the huge waves.
An old man with a cane shuffles ashore.
He has come for me.
He can barely walk.
He can scarcely see.
He is the captain of the boat.

Contemplation

I love the notion of seafaring on the open ocean, but this boat is not big enough for huge ocean waves. This blind, old captain is not my idea of a capable, strong commander. How can he possibly navigate this boat without sight or physical strength? If I go with him, I must give up all notion of control. I will be plunged into the mercy of the wild, perilous current of the night mind's unknown, unfathomable ocean. Is this what a book-writing journey requires? Could this be an initiation dream? How will I ever know unless I set forth?

Angel Benediction

A plump, older woman with angel wings. Her arms are spread wide open toward me.

Contemplation

I don't belong to the devout multitudes who believe in angels… and certainly not the type with wings. But here is a benevolent, buxom, old angelic-winged goddess figure who has come to me in a dream. Why discredit the significance of her presence? I would be a fool to negate her blessing toward my writing life. It is just as reasonable to accept that I have an angel opening her arms to me as to reject her presence as just a dream.… So I will receive her blessing over me and my dream book project.

A Flower Blooms Inside Ayers Rock

I walk through a narrow curved opening
to a cave within Ayers Rock.
Inside,
there is a succulent plant
with a bright red flower.
How does it grow here
in the dark
without sunshine?

Contemplation

Ayers Rock (Uluru) is an island mountain in the Australian outback. It is sacred to the creation mythology of the Aboriginal Dreamtime. It holds the stories, the energy and the vitality of the ancestors. Their creative essence remains forever within this living rock. In my dream, I am inside an underground chamber inside this ancient symbol of the Dreamtime. A bright red blossom opens in darkness. Dreamtime energy seems to be blossoming forth inside the dark cave of my nighttime mind.

I Find a Rosetta Stone

I visit a quaint gallery filled with rare antique artifacts.
There is a display containing a curious stone.
It is a beautiful Rosetta Stone.
It is inscribed with concentric circles.
The gallery owner slips it onto a cord
and places it around my neck.
I imagine owning this exquisite Rosetta Stone.
But the price is far more than I can afford.
And yet somehow,
I stroll out of the gallery
with the Rosetta Stone around my neck,
without paying or being asked to pay.

Contemplation

The Rosetta Stone is an ancient inscribed stone slab with the linguistic key to understanding complex hieroglyphics. But the concentric circles on my dream stone are different from the hieroglyphics on the actual Rosetta Stone. Unlike one single translation, the circles suggest multiple layers of meaning. The placing of a Rosetta Stone around my neck feels like an ordination. I am being called to teach the language of dreams, to help seekers crack the codes of symbolic thought, and unlock the mysterious circular messages embedded in dreams.

Power Surge

I am introduced to an East Indian woman.
She is dressed in a red sari.
She instructs me to hold my hands together
with my thumbs and forefingers connecting into a rectangle.
I feel an electric current pass through my body.
The power surging through me is overwhelming.
She tells me:
Now, you need a bigger book.

Contemplation

My first book (*I Had the Craziest Dream Last Night*) was published with high-key black and white graphics and abbreviated text. Since its publication, I have longed to write a more in-depth book about The DreamingArts. But whenever I set out to do so, the ghost of my insecurity rises and puts psychic barriers in my path. The voices in my head tell me that I am a visual artist, not a writer and that I have no business trying to write a real book. By day, I am beset by doubt. I want to quit writing. But at night, a Hindu woman comes to me as a guide. She instructs me to make the rectangular sign of the book with my opposing hands. This action creates a power surge throughout my body. It is a visceral jolt of energy—a directive. I know for certain now that I must write this book.

Grotto of the Sacred Heart

I visit the underground grotto
of the Sacred Heart.
The path downward is touched
by the sacredness here.
At the bottom of the grotto,
there is an ever-burning fire.
It must be tended.

Contemplation

As a tender of dreams, I must consider my writing a sacred journey. Can I acknowledge that my work in the field of dreams is worthy of reverence? That the path itself is consecrated? That my writing must not be thought of as a laborious intellectual task but a tending of the creative fire burning within the underground chamber of my heart? What force is directing me to face the profound devotion it will take to make this journey as a writer? There is a powerful and eternal fire coming through my dreams sanctifying my passage.

Carrying My Baby

*My old friend is carrying my baby.
She coos and gurgles and sings to it.*

Contemplation

My book is like a precious newborn life. It is being held in the arms of a dear old friend of mine. In the waking world, my friend is an unexceptional writer. But she is an animated, lively mother who knows how to talk yummy baby talk. I need to develop a luscious, juicy voice for my infant first draft. I don't have to care if my writing is "good" or "bad." Only that I nurture my newborn voice.

The Garden Has Begun

The first flower of spring appears.
I bring in the colorful blossom
from its drab winter background.
Then two blooms appear.
The garden has begun.

Contemplation

After a long barren winter of drab writing, my writing style is beginning to blossom.

Blind Man's Owl

I am in a rush!
As I race past a blind man,
I shout I'm in a hurry! I'm graduating!
But he stops me.
He introduces me to a tiny owl on his shoulder.
Would I like to have an owl for a companion?
I slow down. I stop rushing.
I reflect on what it would mean
to have a relationship with an owl.

Contemplation

I am in a hurry to write this book and graduate as a recognized "Master of the Art of Dreams." But an old blind man is standing in my way like the archetypal sightless seers in traditional mythic legends. The blind man recognizes me. He has come to slow me down. He has come to shift my energy. He offers me an owl as a companion. An owl hunts with a vision that pierces through the darkness. It can see things in the night that I can't see. If I accept the owl, I will be the blind one.

If I accept this offer, my relationship with my writing must change. I must stop my ambitious, goal-oriented momentum and my hunger for success. I have been offered an attendant nocturnal emissary of wisdom and ancient knowledge. I can explain this visitation as only a dream. Or I can believe that something outside ordinary waking reality has appeared to guide me. The choice is mine.

Stepping Stones

I am standing beside a large pool of crystal clear water.
There are large stones in the water.
I step over the stones with ease.
I am no longer young and agile enough
to move with fluid speed over the rocks,
but I have enough balance
when I take the time to step slowly.

Contemplation

I cross over the clear primal source from which all forms of life (and books) begin. I am able to move easily over the slippery but solid stepping stones. If I take slow, careful steps and stay balanced, I will be able to write this book one passage at a time.

Where Am I Going?

I am at the gate at the airport.
I have no ticket or boarding pass.
The ticket agent asks
Where am I going?
I don't know.

Contemplation

I am beginning the long journey to get this book project off the ground. There are so many directions it could go in. I don't know where the writing will take me.

Each Step Is Uncertain

I am wandering in a snowy landscape.
Each step is uncertain.
At any moment, I could sink through the ice below.

Contemplation

I am unsettled and meandering through the glacial landscape of my book project. At any moment, my writing could freeze up. I could lose my balance and sink below the surface. This feels like my work pattern: a snowstorm of writing activity followed by that frozen-stiff feeling when my writing momentum inevitably slumps into frigid, icy numbness.

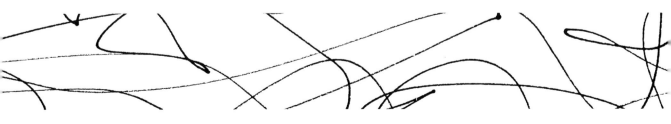

The Blank Page

I throw away
a long white sheet of writing paper.
There is no point in writing upon it.
Why?
Because
I know
sooner or later,
The Nazis will take it away.

Contemplation

This vision of the blank white page taunts me. It represents the oppressive, anxiety-producing agony of the writer's Sturm und Drang. I might as well throw the book project away before I put all my time and energy into it. Even if I push myself to my limits, I know that anything I write will plunge me into self-condemnation and self-defeat. The Nazi threat can impose no more torture than what I can inflict upon myself. I might as well stop writing now.

Boxed-in Whale

A whale is boxed and loaded
on the bottom of a truck bed.
It is bent in half and crushed
under piles of heavy junk.

Contemplation

My book has turned into a whale of a project. It's words of wisdom are confined beneath a lot of useless old mind junk and wasted verbiage. It cannot survive under these present crushing conditions. If I want to save this large body of work and take my book to the next level, I need to lighten the load weighing my writing down. I need to return to the innermost oceanic depths of my creative source where my words and ideas can swim freely.

The Master Conductor

The master conductor cannot go onstage.
He has lost all confidence in himself.
He wears a clownish pointed hat
with an arrow perched on top,
pointing to his brain.
He will only go on stage if he can wear this hat.
I insist that he take it off.
He must accept who he is.
He is not a clown.
He is an accomplished conductor.
But he waits backstage
and waits.

Contemplation

I have lost my confidence that I can orchestrate the many sections of my book project with the excellence in writing and design that is expected of me. I feel inadequate for this task. I don't know how to appear as a respected professional "Master of the Art of Dreams." I need to present myself as a dunce in order to criticize myself before anyone else has a chance.

The High Jump

Outside the door to my studio,
I am going to jump!
I am going to jump very, very high!
I already know precisely how this will feel.
I already know how exhilarating it will be
to look down from such a height!
But I hang back.
I wonder
Should I put on sunscreen?
Then I realize...
there's no point in protecting myself
from the effects of the sun.
The reality is
I really can't jump high at all.

Contemplation

I think I can write this book. I know I can write it. I know how bright the sun will shine on me when I dazzle dreamers with my book once it is published…but now, my self-confidence has collapsed. I have lost faith in myself. I have stopped writing.

Arrested Development

I see a single flower bud
in a vase.
It is not opening.
But it is not dead.
It seems to be in a state
of arrested development.

Contemplation

This bud feels like my book project. It should be about to bloom, but it remains at a standstill. There is no further growth, no development of my manuscript. Instead of blossoming forth, nothing is happening.

I Hit The Wall

I speed down a steep slope
hurtling my body downhill.
To stop my momentum,
I slow myself down
at the bottom of the hill
by hitting a wall.

Contemplation

This is my pattern. Repeatedly, I throw myself into a writing sprint to gain momentum on my book project (my *body* of work), only to stop in my tracks by hitting a wall.

Flying Potato

I discover a flying toy potato.
It floats in the air!
I envision myself painting the potato
with many bright colors!
But then,
it runs out of energy.
This flying toy potato is not meant to carry weight.
Even the weight of the paint
prevents this flying toy potato
from getting off the ground.

Contemplation

I am flying high with colorful, exuberant language for my book. But my writing style is becoming cumbersome with elliptical modes of expression, run-on sentences, absent segues, overloaded verbiage and excessive use of adjectives and semicolons. I am weighed down by impossible expectations. I can't see how my book project will ever get off the ground.

Flooding All Over

The glass door of my washing machine
is off its hinges.
Something is wrong.
I run the machine anyway.
The water floods all over.
There is no way to stop it.

Contemplation

I am spilling over with undisciplined energy. I am flooded with ideas and inspiration. But the mechanism for cleaning up this book project is off its hinges. Despite the signs that my manuscript is not in working order, I am running myself hard.

The Jolt

Standing on a tabletop,
I am probing the socket
of a light bulb
with my tongue.
I ignite myself
with an electrical jolt!

Contemplation

This dream feels like my crazy, intense way of working. Probing an electrical socket with my tongue may not be the best way to connect to my creative writing energy source. There must be another way.

The Spiraling Vortex

I find myself controlled by a spiraling vortex!
A shower of wildness and frenzy!
Hurling myself in all directions!
Endlessly diversifying myself!
Creating more and more patterns and textures!
Filling the world with a storm of color and form!

Contemplation

I am blessed with exuberant energy. I am endlessly diversifying myself. I enthusiastically develop innovative, creative activities for every workshop I teach. I possess an active, animated power that I am genuinely grateful for. Still, my tumultuous style is a counterflow to organizing my thoughts into a coherent linear outline for my book project. I can't seem to get it under control.

It Won't Let Go

A large, furry rodent
jumps on me.
It latches on to my neck.
I try to pry its sharp teeth off my throat.
It won't let go.
It has a grasp on me.

Contemplation

Ambition feels like a rat gnawing mercilessly on my neck with its sharp teeth. I feel ambushed by my relentless, insatiable need for success.

I Miss the Boat

*I find the river,
but I've missed the boat.*

Contemplation

I have found the river of creativity that flows steadily, unfalteringly, and undeniably through me. But it may be too late for me to embark upon this ambitious book project at this late stage of my life. I feel that the ship has sailed without me. I must make peace with the feeling that I might never write this book or achieve all I have aspired to.

Ship of Fools

The sailors on this boat
are a bunch of misfits.
I demand to see the captain.
But there is no one at the helm!!!!
Who is steering this ship?

Contemplation

This boat feels like my book project. There is a crew of undisciplined, indecisive, confused lunatics inside the vessel that is my mind. But what if the misfits are tricksters? Trickster archetypes are often portrayed as mischief-makers and rule-breakers. Are they gleefully poking fun at my sanctimonious writing style? Are they reveling in the sinking of the book as I envision it? On the other hand, this may be my opportunity to add some holy madness, change the rules, throw my self-condemnation overboard, become the captain of my ship and take the helm!

Iridescent Answer

Iridescent pink.
This is the answer to my shitty first draft.
I feel the embarrassment.
I feel the tenderness.

Contemplation

I feel tender and vulnerable about presenting my embryonic manuscript to an editor. I have attempted to make my writing luminous, but I'm afraid I haven't achieved my intended excellence. I feel embarrassed about offering my fragile writing for a critical appraisal. A friend says she thought writers were supposed to start with a "shitty first draft." How could I have forgotten this basic, fundamental reality of book writing?

Big Fish

I catch a massive, big black fish.
Somehow, I drag it home.
But it is so heavy, I can't haul it into the fridge.
If I can't lift it or preserve it or cook it, it will spoil.
My neighbor invites me over.
His kitchen is flooded with radiant light.
His shelves are filled with illuminated glass containers.
I tell him about my big fish.
He lights up!
He will lift and carry the massive fish
into his kitchen.
He will cook it for me.
I am so relieved!

Contemplation

I have caught a fish that is too big for me. This enormous, heavy fish feels like my book project. I can drag it, but it is so heavy I can't lift it. This big book project will spoil if I can't chill it or cook it. It will lose all of its flavor, and it will stink. What am I going to do with it? My book feels like a fish out of water. But to my delight, a helper lives nearby. He will save my project. He has a magical kitchen illuminated with light and transparency to transform my heavy project into a radiant, nutritious feast for my future readers. I have an inner alchemist! He knows how to cook the book!

Admiration

My new apartment is barely settled.
Only a few of my favorite artworks and gifts are unpacked.
The man from next door visits.
He admires each and every object.

Contemplation

This barely-settled apartment feels like my unfinished book. The artwork and gifts seem to represent the book chapters that I have finished writing and designing. An admiring man next door is giving me positive feedback! I may not have finished unpacking the entire book project, but the sections I have written are praiseworthy.

What Was Cramped Is Now Expansive

I am asked to test-drive a car.
It will be challenging to drive while writing my reactions.
A man sits beside me.
I ask him to record my thoughts as I drive.
My first thought is that the car's roof is too low and cramped.
When I look over to see if he is recording my impression,
He is not writing.
He is smiling.
The roof is suddenly very, very high!
The feeling that was cramped is now expansive!

Contemplation

I am testing the worthiness and condition of this vehicle that will carry my writing to the next level. I am steering and controlling this project, but it feels so cramped. My passenger lifts the roof off this limitation. He seems to be a delightfully capricious trickster casting a magical spell. When I awaken, I feel an expansive sense of euphoria. I have found another dream companion to help me drive this project forward.

Buddha Behind Me

The Buddha is walking behind me.

Contemplation

A dominant aspect of Buddhism is understanding the nature of mind. The practice of The DreamingArts is also about understanding the nature of mind. The Buddha is a teacher. I am a teacher. I do not consider myself a Buddhist, but the dream image of Buddha gives me a peaceful sense of being supported by The Awakened One. The Buddha is behind my book project. He's got my back!

The Dalai Lama Strokes My Feet

I visit a Tibetan temple.
I sit by the edge of a pond.
I take off my old work boots.
I put my aching feet in the water.
My feet are gently caressed
by an unseen presence.
The Dalai Lama sits on the other side of the pond.
It is he who has been stroking my feet.
It is his way of having a conversation with me.

Contemplation

I do not consider myself a religious person. I don't have a spiritual practice. I don't follow a guru, a roshi or a rabbi. I do not define myself as a Buddhist. Yet, my dreams are filled with undeniable transcendent guidance. My dreams have a mystical, sacred component instructing and guiding me. When I take off my heavy work boots, the "soles" of my feet are held by an exceptional spiritual leader. He is refreshing my tired and aching "soul" so I can take the next step in my writing life. He is supporting the foundation of my body of work. He is connecting with my soul, energizing, rejuvenating, and restoring me for the work ahead.

Butterflies Out of Darkness

A beautiful black woman comes to stay.
She is magnificent and enchanting.
Without a doubt, she is royalty.
Together,
we climb a steep ladder into the attic.
It is dark and deserted.
I am apprehensive.
She opens the attic doors
to the shadowy space inside.
Exquisite Monarch butterflies
escape into the light.

Contemplation

A beautiful, royal goddess figure comes to me. She leads me into the darkness, opening the door to my dreaming mind's attic. Soulful lifeforms of unspeakable beauty fly out from trunks filled with forgotten writings and old dream journals. Butterflies are creatures of transformation that undergo a metamorphosis from crawling to flying. These dream butterflies feel like beautiful pages in my book that have developed from the slow, crawling caterpillar-like memories, dreams and reflections inside my mind.

My Silky, Long, Dark Hair

I brush out my hair
for the first time
since my new haircut.
When I look in the mirror,
I am astonished.
My hair is so long and dark and beautiful.
It feels so soft and silky.
I am amazed and delighted.

Contemplation

It will feel so good when my book is combed through and edited.

I Snuggle with a Lion

Floating at sea:
I snuggle with a lion
in the hull of a boat.

Contemplation

I am floating gently aboard a dream boat on the open waters of my deep creative source. My dream lion is so soft, so tender. I feel the beat of his heart beneath his savage exterior. I hear him purr. I enfold myself in the intimacy of his mighty presence. My literary lion is embracing me, heart-to-heart, soul-to-soul. His blood is now my blood. His courage is now my courage. His power is now my power. I feel his pulse, power and blood flowing in my book.

Floating Down the River

My dream students have gathered
to float down the river
in a small boat.
We all are in good spirits.
The river is full and flowing!
The water is crystal clear!
We are merry!
We are enjoying the outing.
The boat carries a box
with everything we need
for a complete workshop experience.

Contemplation

My book is flowing toward completion. It holds everything I want to offer to my students and readers. My book will be completed in joy. And it will be good!

Serving the Dalai Lama

I am called to make tea for the Dalai Lama.
My teacups are all cracked and broken.
But they are all that I have.
So they are what I will use
to serve.

Contemplation

I am offered an extraordinary opportunity to serve tea to a holy, spiritual guide. I never doubt that I can make the tea, but I am humbled by my inability to present it in a perfect container. Could my work be anything but cracked and flawed before His Excellence? I must put my need for perfectionism aside and publish the book that I have been called to write. Despite my flaws, I can serve the world of dreamers and seekers. My book will be refreshing as a stimulating cup of tea, and although flawed, it will be enough.

Dreams are illustrations from the book your soul is writing about you.
Marsha Norman

PART III
CAPTURE YOUR DREAMS

The Dream Journal

I should advise you to put it all down as beautifully as you can – in some beautifully bound book. It will seem that you are making the visions banal – but then you need to do that – then you are freed from the power of them…Then when these things are in some precious book, you can go to the book and turn over the pages, and for you, it will be your church – your cathedral – the silent places of your spirit where you will find renewal. If anyone tells you that it is morbid or neurotic and you listen to them – then you will lose your Soul – for that book is your Soul.

C. G. Jung

Keeping a dream journal can take many forms, including riffs, ruminations and contemplations of memories, musings, and meditations. In the next two chapters, I share a range of journal techniques to explore the intriguing tales woven by the night mind. My intention is to support you in your conversation with Psyche and to acquaint you with the language of your dreams. I don't presume to be prescriptive, to give you a formula or to tell you how to analyze your dreams. I will not tell you what a star is, but I will advocate for stargazing. I will not map the contours of the ocean, but I will urge you to set out to sea. However, I will encourage you to experiment with a variety of creative approaches that invite your imagination to run wild about matters that touch your heart.

Traces of the Journey

Choose an appealing blank book to hold observations, impressions and discoveries from your expedition into the inner world. Regard it as a repository for your rantings, ravings, confessions, prayers and promises. Use it as a ledger to record your challenges, setbacks and successes. Treat it as an archive for your collages, sketches, photos, poems and paintings. As time passes, your journal will transform into a precious collection of your Conversations with Psyche.

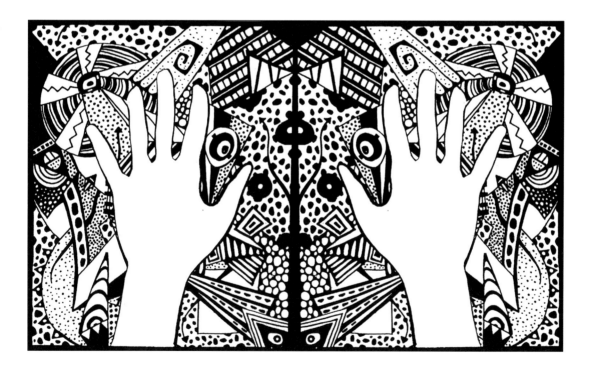

Weave a Net of Intention

Dreams come to us every night, whether we remember them or not. In the morning light of consensus reality, most dreams evaporate the instant we awaken. Dreams are like gossamer strands, always on the verge of trailing out just beyond conscious awareness. Dream memory is short, details are lost, and punchlines disappear. They can vanish into thin air as if we never dreamt at all. They fade away when we look at them too directly or try to pin them down. They are so slick, so wiggly, so eager to escape.

Because dreams are quick to dematerialize, you must be just a tad quicker. Before you go to bed, place a tiny night light, a pen and your journal or voice-activated recorder beside your bed so you are prepared to record a dream whenever you catch one. Upon waking, wait in stillness. Search for a telltale thread. When you recall a dream or a dream fragment, record it as soon as possible. At first, you may only sense a glimmer of a dream, like a shadowy presence hovering just beyond your perception. Write down any wisps or impressions, no matter how small or faint: a color, a sensation, a voice, an emotion. Don't despair if only a hint of a dream is in your net. It is rarely possible to capture a whole dream. Welcome whatever you catch, however trivial or nonsensical it may seem; record it without censure. You may be unable to discern its significance by first impressions and appearances. Still, as you experiment with the DreamingArts techniques in this book, you will find that every dream or fragment is more expressive than you imagined.

Dreams are elusive and ephemeral, but the more you record them, the more they appear. Psyche tends to speak when she knows she'll be heard. Dream journaling will signal Psyche that you are paying attention. Your job is to flirt with her, entice her, embrace her, and invite her to converse with you. Whisper to her every night before you fall asleep. Cast your net. Then, be patient. Psyche usually comes when called, but she comes in her own time, not on demand.

Incubation

If you are wrestling with an issue or problem, you may want to compose a dream incubation before you go to sleep. Set your intention by writing out a query in your journal, but suspend judgment about the message you receive. Asking a question does not mean Psyche will give you a direct answer. Her response may show up in the form of a sphinx-like reply. You will most likely receive a puzzle, a metaphor or a koan. DreamingArts techniques can help you sift down through your dreams' enigmatic layers until you awaken to what they are telling you.

Create a Ceremony

Entering your dreamwork through the DreamingArts is like embarking on a pilgrimage. It is respectful to begin each journal session with a blessing. Light a candle, ring a bell, recite an invocation, read your dream. Invite the spirits that hover through the nightscape to step into your waking life.

An Invocation

May the dream candle I now kindle
inspire me
to use my intuition, my power and my delight;
To sing the songs of my loves, my sorrows,
my light and my losses;

To heal, to bless, to create;
To reveal the gifts of the spirit of the dream
within me.

Getting Started

There are no rules. Here they are…
— *Scott McCloud*

As soon as you wake up, write down anything about your dream you can recall in your journal. Your conscious mind will likely protest: I don't remember enough! There is nothing worth capturing in this dream! This dream makes no sense! There is too much; I'll never catch it all! Acknowledge these protests, but write anyway.

Train yourself to write down whatever you can, whether sketchy or nonsensical. Start with modest intentions. You probably will not be able to catch a whole dream. Make a note of shards, fragments, close encounters or anything that glimmers. It can be the recollection of a single object, a word, a color, a song title or a jingle; it can be an impression or a feeling. It can be a quick sketch. Avoid the temptation to judge either the dream's merit or your description's completeness. Go with whatever wants to come forth, even if it doesn't seem to make sense…especially if it doesn't! Wisps of sensations are okay! Remnants of vague impressions are okay! Crazy mixed-up nonsense is okay! Indulge in whatever kind of language the dream wants to express, whether formal, jargon or slang. Resist the urge to editorialize or change any initial misspellings or grammar. Idiosyncratic wordings and misspellings can all be clues to Psyche's intention.

Report: Re-Read Your Dream Notes, Fill Out the Details

When you have time to settle down with your journal, re-read your sketchy dream notes and fill in missing details. Your conscious mind will likely protest: I don't remember more! But if you give yourself over to the process and begin to annotate, rewrite or type up your dream, you will discover that you do tend to remember more. It is extremely rare to remember a dream in its entirety, but you will often remember more than you think. Write your dream in the first person, present tense, as if it is happening now.

Record the Date of Your Dream

A date keeps your dreams in chronological order. When you look back into your journals, the dates will help you track how your dreams have evolved.

Give Your Dream a Title

A title condenses a dream's essential message into a few words. It highlights a significant characteristic or distills a theme in a concise phrase. Dreams are rarely about one thing, so if you like, give the dream subtitles, emphasizing different aspects of the dream. This simple task will embed the dream into your waking consciousness, even if you have no more time to attend to it.

Your Life Log

The events of your life fill your dreams, often shaping their context. Keeping a Life Log in your dream journal helps pinpoint the people and events that may have influenced your dreams. Jot down notes about what you were doing, thinking and feeling in the day(s) before your dream. Major incidents, as well as minor happenings, will yield unexpected clues, connections and associations.

A Museum of Moons. Tarantula Coat. The Elusive Meatloaf. Euphorbian Dinosaurs. The House Is Leaking Poems. A Dying Monkey Guru. A Double-Headed Snake Dog. Baby Inside a Milk Cow. Fish-Eyed Vampire. The Road of the Tiny Ghosts. A Flight Path for Dragons. Rabbit In a Wedding Dress. I Can See Through the Wall. Weird Doings with Smoke. A Constant State of Wafflement. Where the Edible Bibles Are Printed. Performance by a Pet Fish. A Wild Mane of Shaggy Pink Hair. Aquatic Prairie Dog. A Bleeding Rainbow. A Lion In My Backyard. Baby Gone Wild. A Flower Blooms In the Dark. My New Lover Comes Home. Drawn to the Sun. A Delicate Balance. The Pieces Fit Together. The Shy Cat Comes Out of The Cave. A Gathering of Women. Extraordinary Ellie. I Drink the Sweet Nectar.

DreamLexicon: Anatomy of the Dream

….a treasure map to the deep self
—Clarissa Pinkola Estés

Building Blocks

Every dream is a puzzle created from component parts that make up the intricate montage of each nighttime narrative. It is helpful to separate individual images by creating a Dream Lexicon in your journal. Take a few minutes to list the people, creatures, inanimate objects, settings and actions in your dream. Describe or sketch each image. Look up definitions and synonyms for unusual words and pithy phrases. Research literary, mythological and archetypal references. Take note of the differences between the appearance of images in your waking reality versus those in your dreams. Notice the ways each motif evokes emotions, memories and associations.

Once you have deconstructed your dream into elemental parts, select the most intriguing dream images to use as writing prompts for five-minute sprints or free-association morning pages. Pretend you are an observer from another culture or planet with no knowledge of the physical world, the people who appear, or the customs of your community. Keep a wide-open beginner's mind. Let your stream-of-consciousness flow. Invite your thoughts to percolate without directing them with your rational mind. Notice how your descriptions of each image start to reveal insights into your dream as you riff, ruminate and contemplate.

In Part V, I have used a dream about my dog, "Molly Dog Returns," to demonstrate how I have developed a Dream Lexicon. As you read the following chapter, you can toggle back and forth to compare each lexicon entry with its Molly Dream example.

Dream Characters

Dreams present a diverse cast of characters, each capable of triggering a range of emotions from tenderness to terrifying. Dream beings come in the guise of comrades, villains, pranksters and guides. They may be familiar family members, co-workers, childhood friends, teachers or significant others from different times of our lives. They may be well-known celebrities or complete strangers. They may appear as a composite of two seemingly unrelated people. They often display peculiar, uncharacteristic, outlandish or atypical traits. Dream characters have a profound effect on us and bring up a multitude of feelings, flashbacks and associations.

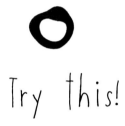

In your Dream Lexicon, list each character that appears in your dream, including your dream self. Whether familiar or unfamiliar, take note of distinctive physical attributes, behavioral qualities, and personality traits. If your characters are a fusion of two people, describe their individual qualities as well as their combined features. Observe how each character influences the direction of the dream. There is an intrinsic connection between all living beings, both in the outer world and the imaginal world of dreams. Consider how each dream character mirrors your connections to waking life relationships. Pay attention to the emotions and memories that are evoked.

My Hostile Lover. The Wobbly Warriors. A Dangerous Baby. Dinner With Elvis. The Defiant Prostitute. Two Fools. Extraordinary Annie. My Bull-Headed Roommate. An Angelic Entity. A Combustible Conductor. Lunar Relief Widows. A Woman of Substance. A Tired Old Showgirl. The Scowling Nun. A Homeless Vagrant. My Suave Salsa Teacher. The Belligerent Twins. The Mango Princess. A Formidable Enemy. An Old Sad Man. My Restless Mother. A Nazi Tormentor. An Extraneous Wife. The Hungry Squatter. The Secret Perpetrator. The Playful Dominatrix. The Queen's Inspector. A Man With No Feet. A Dying Daughter. The Rebel Renegade. The Aspiring Escape Artist. A Savage Scoundrel. Three Flamboyant Sisters. An Author on the Run. A Sneak Thief in the Water Tower. Romeo Without Juliet.

Dream Creatures

As humans, we share a special bond with the diverse creatures that inhabit our planet and the intricate web of our dreams. Dream animals come in various forms that mimic real or imaginary life forms. They may appear as a combination of different animals or possess human-like qualities. They may range from domestic to wild, predator to prey, endangered to extinct, exhibiting a range of behaviors from gentle playfulness to ferocious aggressiveness. Behind each animal are archetypal attributes, ancient mysteries and mystical powers that link us to our fundamental, instinctive nature.

Create a list of the dream animals and creatures in your Dream Lexicon. Describe their physical attributes, behavior, and temperament. Observe the way they move. Notice how they engage with their environment. Become aware of the similarities and differences between their appearance in both the dream state and the waking world. Dream animals communicate with us through their presence and wisdom. They foster a deep connection with the untamed facets of our primal selves. As you align with the spirit of your dream animal, record the feelings and recollections that their traits bring forth.

Aquatic Prairie Dogs. A Package of Six Baby Bengal Tigers. Neglected Rattlesnake. Stepping on Dragons. A Lion In My Backyard. A Chicken-Headed Coyote. The Blue Raccoons. Euphorbian Dinosaurs. A Bucking Mechanical Horse. Bunny on a Leash. Tarantula Bite. The Dog-Headed Snake. Almost a Poodle. A Scorpion With Human Eyes. Monkey Man. Mischievous Water Horse. A Toad With Copper Claws. The Three-Legged Tiger Is Loose. Wild Sea Dogs. A Rabbit in a Wedding Dress. Wingless Worn Out Sand Bird. Cardboard Butterflies. Piglet Escapes. Every Boy Should Have a Lizard. A Horse With a White Wound. A Fish With the Head of a Hawk. Man-Eating Marsupials. Unleashed Bird People. Stranded Sea Goats. Albino Dachshund With Pestilent Breath. A Skinless Sea Serpent. King of Reptiles. Dining With Irritable Gators and Horse Goblins.

Dream Objects

Inanimate objects hold as much significance as the living entities we encounter in our dreams. Every thingamajig, doohickey, gadget and gizmo is a revealing prop that exerts a meaningful presence. Inorganic images range from material items like conveyances, contraptions, mechanisms and machinery to curios, costumes, accessories and artifacts. How things function, what condition they are in, and what they are worth all have a bearing on the impressions and associations they conjure up.

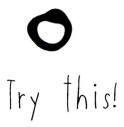

Try this!

Make a list of the inanimate objects in your Dream Lexicon. Enumerate their physical attributes and catalog their intended purpose, design, and value. Observe their shape, size, color, texture and condition. Compare how your dream objects function in the waking world with the peculiar, extraordinary or unconventional way they operate in your dream. Notice if the language you use to describe lifeless objects corresponds to predicaments and quandaries in your waking life.

This Ancient Book. The Big Train is Here. A Dazzling Yellow Chicken Outfit. The Retractable Hem. The Elusive Meat Loaf. A Tangled Thread. Thick Oily Black Fire Balls. A Bag of Dirt. Spoiled Milk. I Need a Gun. The Whole Tooth. Lavish Clouds of Guano. A Flying Toy Potato. Stones Too Heavy to Move. Miracle Mayonnaise. Dependable Old Lazy Boy. An Airplane Ticket With No Destination. A Flame Deep Down Inside. Overcooked Glue Pot. Immense Stone Goddess. Houseboat on the Plaza. A Block of Marble Dust. A Pool Filled With Hot Needles. A Crooked Silver Rainbow. A Vial of Iridescent Healing Herbs. A Bucking Mechanical Horse. The Tarnished Helmet. Lopsided Sand Mandala. My Headache Headband. A Spear and a Shield. Your Kimono From the Sea. A Shaggy Shroud of Many Colors.

Dream Actions

Dreams allow us to experience extraordinary happenings and behave in uncommon ways. They often feature gripping storylines filled with thrilling escapades, harrowing struggles and peculiar encounters. Whether we're soaring through the sky, crawling on all fours, battling foes, fleeing from danger, wandering aimlessly, or busting a move on the dance floor, dreams serve as a reminder of the limitless challenges and possibilities that reside within us.

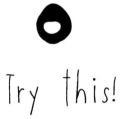

Try this!

In your Dream Lexicon, isolate the actions, events, activities and exploits in your dream. Identify any conflicts or confrontations that arise. Notice where the narrative shifts, repeats a pattern, falls into an endless loop or stops abruptly. Observe how the obstacles and transitions in your dreams reflect the interactive state of affairs and existential questions you may face in your waking life.

Escaping From the Fake Investigation. Barreling Down the Highway. Hurling Myself Into the Deep Chasm. Playing With Action Figures. Swinging on a Twisted Rope. Floating Above Still Waters. Refusing the High Dive. Dripping With Blood. Running Out of Gas. Crawling Out of the Ooze. Driving Blind. Slipping on Ice. Swarming With Bees. Nursing the Unknown Babe. Wading In Toxic Runoff. Breaking the Slender Thread. Spiraling Into the Vortex. Running Out of Energy. Clinging to Dust Balls. Clowning Around in Red Santa Pants. Jumping Down From the High Ledge. Unleashing Hungry Monsters. Rescuing Elephants. Taking the Bait. Failing the Entrance Exam. Dancing With Abandon. Deactivating the Armed Forces. Crushing the Tender Filaments. Pushing the Planet Beyond Space and Time.

DreamScapes

The dreamscape is where the plot of a dream materializes. Every dream has a unique environment, giving it a distinct mood and ambiance. The landscape, architecture, vegetation, and atmosphere all play significant roles. Within the dream life, there is no separation between our minds, our bodies and the spaces we inhabit. Wastelands and depleted landscapes can reflect our physical and emotional suffering, while lush, fertile panoramas align with our physical and emotional well-being. The setting of a dream attunes us to the spirit of our outer and inner life.

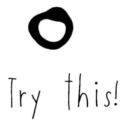

Try this!

Isolate the various dream scenes and settings in your Dream Lexicon. Provide details about the location, weather, and time of day. Be mindful of the quality of the light, the topography and the plant life. Notice the entrances, exits, intersections, and connections. Make a note of the obstacles, barriers, dividers and dead ends. Observe how the environment in your dreams reflects the physical and emotional grounding in your waking life.

The Grotto of The Sacred Heart. Madhouse Jail. A Flight Path for Dragons. The World's Control Center. Trail to the Bear's Lair. The Precarious Approach to the Bottomless Pit. Don't Look Under the Bridge. A Chance To Go Backstage. A Room Filled With Fishes. The Basement is Flooded With Radiant Light. An Underground Fire Station. Quicksand Ahead. Stepping Stones Over a Muddy, Soggy Swamp. The Pool Where the Tigers Swim at Night. Encroaching Fires at the Water's Edge. Nighttime Navigation Through a Dangerous Tunnel. Tumultuous Squall Where the Flood Has Receded. A Crystal Clear Pool of Water. Lost in the Soggy Darkness. A Breakthrough in the Surface Ice. The End of the Great Pollen Pathway. A Landscape of Layer Cakes. The Slippery Road to the Forest of Thorns. The Illuminated Metropolis of the Stone Goddess.

Questions

Dreams come to us as riddles filled with enigmatic imagery, odd encounters, eccentric characters, obscure references and paradoxical imagery. They haunt us with reverberations of the unknown and the unfathomable. But analyzing or interpreting this strange dream world isn't always necessary. Simply notice that you are in a lopsided world that doesn't obey logical rules.

Curiosity is the most valuable resource for unraveling implausible scenarios and perplexing riddles presented by the dreaming mind. Become an investigative journalist. List a series of questions in your Dream Lexicon about the peculiarities in your nighttime narrative. Ask the essential questions of Who, What, Where, When, Why, and How. Your questions may not lead to concrete answers. Simply allow yourself to simply wonder and ruminate about the intriguing puzzles that arise.

What I Will Do With a Two-Headed Baby? How Can I Climb Out of This Hole? Why Is My Owl Named Moses? Why Are These Scorpions Homeless? How Will I Know Which Evening Gown To Wear? Why Is the Toilet Overflowing? Where is Mother Teresa Taking Me? Why Did I Kill My Brother? How Will I Find Elvis? Why am I Scowling at the Squat Old Man? Why Does My Mother Come Back to Life? What Kind of Critters Are Hiding Here? Why Has My Flight Been Canceled? How Will I Find the Nuclear Button? Why is the Back Door Locked? How Did I Become a Child Again? Why Do I Need To Be Rescued? Why Don't I Want to See What's Buried Here? Where Have the Ghosts Gone? Why Does Jerry Go to Jail? How Did I Lose My Purse Again? Where is the Mechanical Failure? How Can I Return to the Sunny Side? Why Is the Basement Window Broken?

Emotions

Dreams are the repository of our deepest feelings. They call to us from the innermost center of our being. They touch us in our tenderest places with the depth of our longing, sorrows and joys. They enchant us with euphoria, arouse our passions, taunt us with jealousy and envelop us in heartbreak. Emotions are the very stuff of dreams. Giving voice to these emotions allows our dreams to reflect our unspoken proclivities and propensities.

Try this!

In your Dream Lexicon, list the range of emotions stirred up by your dream. Re-experience the feelings and sentiments by letting your words tumble and flow without judgment or filter. Allow your heart to burst open and overflow onto the page. Write in an impassioned voice filled with desire, energy and rawness. Use evocative vocabulary. Dare to make judgments. Reveal regrets. Rant about injustices. Surrender to the turbulence of passion, the overflowing of love and the confession of your tenderest feelings. Pour your heart out.

I Feel Threatened by the Monsters and Their Mothers. I Feel Relieved After the Hurricane Has Lost Its Power. I Feel Terrified as I Approach My Execution. I Feel Helpless as I'm Sucked Down the Shower Drain. I Feel Trapped When Surrounded by a Fleet of Destroyers. I Feel Lonely as My Life Force Is Oozing Out. I Feel Confused Over the Unnecessary Death of the Questionable Surgeon. I Feel Euphoric When I Dance With Abandon. I Feel Annoyed by the Squatting Man Wearing a Pointy Green Hat. I Feel Frightened When My Internal Organs Start to Shut Down. I Feel Foolish When I Walk Naked Onto the Podium. I Feel Triumphant When I Set Sail Without Knowing How. I Feel Calm and Serene When I Nurse the Unknown Babe. I Feel Remorseful When I Haven't Defended Myself. I Feel Bitter and Acidic. I Feel Abandoned in My Grief. I Feel Intoxicated in My Moment of Conversion.

Memories

Dreams take us on a journey through concentric rings of time. They lead us in circles, back to all we thought we had left behind. They revive sweet memories and uncover phantoms from the long-ago corners of our lives. Dreams encompass a blend of moments from our personal history: the different homes we lived in, the schools we attended, the jobs we once had and the people we encountered. They feature childhood friends, distant relatives, and those we lost, loved, or loathed. Dreams mix up the fragments, shards and tesserae of our lives into strange and unexpected combinations.

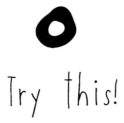

Create a catalog of memories in your Dream Lexicon evoked by your dream. Unwind confusing chronological or sequential time lapses by isolating individual experiences from different periods of your life. Allow your memories to stir up long-forgotten emotions of loneliness, loss, regret, disappointment, pleasure, tenderness, joy and warmth. Ruminate on how past events impact the relationships in your current waking life.

I Remember My Blood Running Cold. I Remember Biting My Tongue. I Remember Running out of Gas. I Remember The Crackling Sounds of the City. I Remember Being Scared Witless. I Remember Smashing a Teapot. I Remember the Fighting in the Streets. I Remember Floating on the Surface of the Lake. I Remember Tasting My First Cup Of Spirits. I Remember My Insatiable Mother. I Remember Playing in the Deep Snow. I Remember Stealing Apples. I Remember Searching for My Lost Wallet. I Remember Hiding From My Brother. I Remember Jumping Into the River Fully Dressed. I Remember Brimming Over With Joy. I Remember Rushing for the Night Train. I Remember Diving Into the Shallow End. I Remember Failing the Test I Remember My Grandfather's Voice. I Remember My Fuzzy Old PussyCat.

This dream world is not your prison; it's your playground.

Robert Moss

PART IV
DREAM JOURNAL TECHNIQUES

Touching the Source

"I will take the Ring," he said, "though I do not know the way."
J.R.R. Tolkien

In this chapter, you will find DreamingArts journal projects, activities and techniques designed to spark your creativity and guide your dream journey. Each method is designed to coax Psyche out of hiding. Each will lead to unanticipated discoveries and insights. When you take the time to unravel the riddles of the night, you will peel back the layers of metaphor, mystery and magic they contain, and you will be amazed by what emerges. The DreamingArts will transform your dreams with wonder and awe where your imagination will thrive and insights will flow.

The following chapter is divided into five sections: DreamWriting, DreamPoetry, DreamingArts, DreamTheater and DreamJourneys. Each section contains its own creative prompts. These are not necessarily meant to be done in the order presented. Feel free to browse through them and try whichever ones pique your interest. If one activity isn't working, skip it and try something else. Experiment, play, mix and match.

When it comes to dream journal sessions, there is no one-size-fits-all approach. You have the freedom to customize your journal according to your preferences and what sparks your imagination. Depending on your schedule, you can opt for short five-minute sprints, long morning pages or rambling midnight meditations. You don't need to know where your dreamwork journey will take you; your rational mind doesn't need to set a goal or be in control. There is no perfect way to do this, so relax and follow the threads wherever they lead.

Trust Yourself

What you do not know is the only thing you know....

T. S. Eliot

Choose the exercises that call to you. Select activities that inspire you to find your own way. Consider these suggestions as your creative dream playground. The DreamingArts are more about discovery than invention. Surrender to the prompts. Trust the process. Trust Psyche. Trust yourself. Let your creativity flow.

Pour Your Heart Out

Your visions will become clear only when you can look into your own heart.

C. G. Jung

The DreamingArts are not concerned with skill or technique but with finding an impassioned, authentic voice—your voice—one that is genuinely alive, responsive and uniquely you. If you let imagination surrender to nocturnal explorations, your dreamwork will be spontaneous and impulsive, filled with energy, courage and intimacy. Your journal will become a powerful tool that allows you to express your opinions, voice your concerns, mourn your failures, celebrate your achievements, embrace your desires, and share your innermost thoughts and feelings.

Authenticity

The big question is whether you are going to be able to say a hearty yes to your adventure.

Joseph Campbell

While plumbing the depths of your dreams through the exercises in this book, try not to think about how your dreamwork might look or sound to others. This is for your eyes only. If you don't want anyone else to know what you have written, keep your journal under lock and key or tucked away in a password-protected computer file. No one but you need ever see or hear what you have created unless you choose to share it. Let go of expectations. Suspend judgments. Your writings and artworks don't need to be masterful or polished. Try not to limit or censor yourself. If you feel you must do so, you can always edit what you share with others. Your task is to silence your inner critic and write intimately, honestly and unrestrained. Use your dream journal to spill your heart out with raw authenticity. Abandon yourself to everything that has been locked inside.

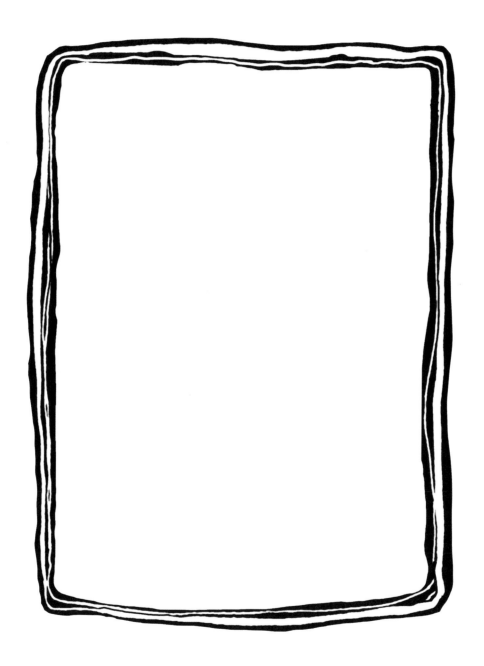

Overcoming Writer's/Artist's Block

The winds of grace are blowing all the time. You have only to raise your sail.

Ramakrishna Paramahansa

Horror Vacui is a Latin term for fear of the blank page. It can overwhelm you when you sit at your desk and stare at an empty piece of paper… and nothing happens. Every creative person knows the feeling. However, putting pen to paper and jotting down even the smallest dream fragment, phrase or sketch can serve as a powerful tool to overcome writer's/artist's block. From the moment you first record a dream, you have material to engage your interest and curiosity. Every dream image carries a prompt that inspires a response. You have eliminated the blankness staring back at you, and by extension, you have broken writer's/artist's block. Recording a dream will automatically launch you into your journaling, writing and art-making practice. Once you transcribe a dream, details will follow, memories will tumble out, and emotions will pour forth. Whatever you have captured will be a springboard for prose, poetry, artmaking, theater pieces, songwriting and dance. You will easily move from belabored conscious thought to a heightened state of effortless concentration, calm and flow. Your creativity will burst forth with unpremeditated intention, building momentum, developing force and spreading like wildfire. No matter how blocked you feel, dreams provide an endless awakening of the dormant energies within.

1
DreamWriting

A dream can be a literary product of startling subtlety, building suspense, tangling its characters in subplots, all created as if by a master author, to spring an exquisitely set trap of revelation. The plasticity of language — semantic backflips, neologisms, and other linguistic legerdemain — can be nothing short of breathtaking.

Mark Barasch

DreamWriting takes you out of your analytical mind and into the imaginative realm, where you can write about impossibilities with authority because you have encountered alternate states of being. Waking world distinctions between the ordinary and the extraordinary don't matter in the world of dreams. Free from the burden of logical thought, you can shout a hearty YES! to your unbridled imagination. In the following section, explore dream imagery that confounds and confuses you. Experiment with various literary forms and styles. Intermingle prose with poetic patterns or simply write out lists of feelings or memories evoked by your dream. Shift voices by writing from different points of view. Give yourself permission to write about irrational, impossible things. The rational mind may not know how to respond to dreams, but the creative self jumps at the chance to wander through the labyrinthine mysteries of Psyche's messages.

The Grotto of The Sacred Heart. Madhouse Jail. A Flight Path for Dragons. The World's Control Center. Trail to the Bear's Lair. The Way to the Bottomless Pit. Don't Look Under the Bridge. A Chance To Backstage. A Room Filled with Fishes. chen is Flooded with Radian Underground Station Above Groun ksand Ahead. Stepping Stones Over Soggy Swamp. Where the Tigers Swim Encroaching Fires at the Water's E htime Navigation Through a Dangerou Tumultuous Squall. The Flood Has Re rystal Clear Pool of Water. Lost ss. Surface Ice. The Night the Earth Shook

Dreams and the Writer Within
Techniques to Inspire Your Expressive Voice

He played with the idea and grew willful; tossed it into the air and transformed it; let it escape and recaptured it; made it iridescent with fancy and winged it with paradox.

Oscar Wilde

In response to activities in this chapter, I have used one dream, "Molly Dog Returns," to demonstrate how a single dream can contain a multitude of varied interpretations. As you read through the following activities, you can toggle back and forth to compare each project here with its Molly Dream example in Part V.

The Five Senses

The mind gathers information about the external material world through the faculties of sound, sight, smell, taste and touch. Describing dream images using vivid sensory details deepens the physical experience of the dream. Sensory awareness awakens emotional responses while enriching the vocabulary with juicy writing.

Try this!

With the assistance of a thesaurus, find a range of expressive adjectives to describe the images in your dream. Embellish the characteristics of your dream beings and enhance the qualities of your dreamscapes with elaborate sensory details. Take note of the sounds, inhale the aromas, savor the flavors, feel the textures and observe the colors. Annotate your dream by activating it with an explosion of the senses.

A Letter

The art of letter writing is a timeless and respected way of communicating carefully considered messages regarding family matters, catching up on gossip with friends, connecting with loved ones, or expressing gratitude. Letters can take various forms ranging from festive salutations, amorous missives, poison pen notes or "Dear John" letters.

Try this!

Compose an emotive letter addressed to one of your dream entities. Your writing style can be sentimental, plaintive, confidential or tear-jerking. Let your heart bleed onto the page. Let your emotions guide you to express yourself in a manner that feels genuine and authentic.

Deconstruction and Reconstruction

The literal transcription of a dream seldom tells the whole story. Night visions are rich with paradox and innuendo. When you replace every dream image with a different word or phrase, meaningful connections appear unexpectedly. Semantic and idiomatic variations provide subtle distinctions that open a dream story without "analyzing" it. This is an uncomplicated way to decode the night's messages before turning to symbol books for dream interpretation.

Try this!

Deconstruct your dream by breaking it down into a list that separates each dream being, object, action, setting, and emotion. Isolate the qualities or characteristics of every dream image by describing each with a few words.

After you have deconstructed your dream narrative, put it back together again. Replace each image, action and emotion with an alternative or equivalent expression. Reconstruct the entire narrative with different word choices for each dream image. Write another version of your dream without using the original vocabulary or wording.

Harangue

Bullies, tyrants, demons and monsters often torment and intimidate us in our nightmares. They come to terrify us in the form of overbearing authoritarians, aggressive taskmasters, domineering slave drivers and oppressive bogeymen. We wake up quaking in fear, unnerved with anxiety or cowering with powerlessness. But we can retrieve our power when we fight back against nightmarish figures with vitriol in our voices.

Try this!

With the sharp edge of your tongue, rip into one of your edgiest dream images. In a threatening and accusatory soliloquy, let your true feelings explode in a stream-of-consciousness tirade. Release your rage and aggression! Hurl retorts or insults! Put an acidic, intense sting in your words and throw your most poisonous barbs! Rant and rave with no fear of consequences or recriminations! Be fearless, insulting, annoying, rude and insane! Defy your villains, stand up and defend yourself! Go ballistic! Beat the odds! Escape from the inescapable! Triumph over conflict! Confront your inner bully!

2
Dream Poetry

Genuine poetry can communicate before it is understood.

T.S. Eliot

Poetry is the form of human language that is closest to the language of dreams. By their very nature, poems are symbolic and impressionistic. Dreams and poetry both inhabit the in-between, non-linear spaces, the interstices of consciousness. Both are a bit feral, made of particles and waves. They dance in and out of being, playing hide-and-seek with your rational mind. When you reenter the dream landscape through poetry, you converse with Psyche in her own lyrical tongue. Poetry can unearth kernels of truth that lie just beyond conscious understanding and can serve as an evocative mode of dream rendering.

To write your dream as a poem, it is not necessary to first interpret or understand it; your task is only to attend to it and to invite it to open and express itself. Restructuring a dream narrative with line breaks slows the action down, converting the storyline into a series of snapshots that separate the dream into component parts. Instead of a motion picture, you have a series of still frames. Without seeking an interpretation of your dream, something profound happens. Meaningful phrases pop into view. The poetic form illuminates the dream by giving keywords and phrases more punch and impact.

Experiment with poetic styles. Write in a freewheeling verse or a more formal structure with or without fixed lines, rhyme or meter. Hyperbolize your writing with heightened imagery, exaggeration and euphemism. Use expanded vocabulary culled from notes in your Dream Lexicon. Mimic your favorite poets, copy their styles or steal their lines! Use word-rhyming dictionaries. Play with the sounds of assonance, dissonance, alliteration, onomatopoeia, cacophony and repetitive language.

Don't worry if you don't consider yourself to be a "Poet." You do not need to be an accomplished writer to do this practice. DreamWriting is not about literary mastery or proficiency; it is simply about getting your thoughts on the page. Dream poetry helps illuminate your dream's meaning by sharpening your focus. Often, after transcribing a dream by adding line breaks, a rhythm reveals itself with a poetic cadence that brings the dream alive. As if by magic, you may find that the poem has written itself.

Dreams and the Poet Within
Techniques to Inspire Your Poetic Voice

*People who look for symbolic meaning fail to grasp
the inherent poetry and mystery of the images.*

René Magritte

In response to activities in this chapter, I have used one dream, "Molly Dog Returns," to demonstrate how a single dream can contain a multitude of varied interpretations. As you read through the following activities, you can toggle back and forth to compare each project here with its Molly Dream example in Part V.

Free Verse

Free-verse poems have no fixed rhythms or patterns of rhyme. Instead, punctuation and stanza breaks emphasize the impact of a dream's recorded words, resulting in a more powerful expression of ideas. This format is well-suited for effortlessly poeticizing dreams without being constrained by formal rules.

Try this!

When putting your dream into a free verse form, use line breaks and punctuation marks to separate your sentences. Remove unnecessary details, imprecise adjectives, generalizations, or wordy explanations. Instead, opt for selecting a few evocative phrases that capture the most dramatic or vivid moments in your dream.

BlackOut Poetry

BlackOut Poetry, also known as Erasure Poetry, is a form of found poetry created by removing portions of a written text and converting the remaining words into an abbreviated composition. By eliminating unnecessary and extraneous words, the focal point of a dream can be concentrated into a simple yet revealing poem.

Try this!

To distill the essence of your dream, highlight or underline the most compelling words and concise phrases in a written account of your dream. Cross out or black out everything else. Arrange your extracted words into lines and stanza breaks until you arrive at a meaningful poetic condensation of your dream's theme.

List Poem

A list poem is a simple format that shapes your writing by repeating the opening line. Rather than adhering to conventional rhymes and poetic metrics, it aims to create a rhythmic flow through the repetition of the opening line.

Try this!

To capture your dream as a list poem, begin each line with the same phrase.

"In this dream, I am…"

Switch identities with each of your dream beings, inanimate objects and dreamscapes. Shift your point of view. Take on the personality of each of your images. Let go of who you think you are. Become empty of intention or ego. Become one with everyone and everything in the dream.

"In this dream, I am…"
"In this dream, I am…"
"In this dream, I am…"
"In this dream, I am…"
"In this dream, I am…"
"In this dream, I am…"
"In this dream, I am…"

Ode

An ode is a type of lyrical poem that is meant to honor and eulogize someone that the poet loves. It often expresses a deeply emotional and exalted feeling. It uses melodic language to glorify a profound experience.

Try this!

Create a rhapsodic poem in the voice of one of your beloved dream characters. Assume an identity that deviates from your own. Write in consistent four-line stanzas with a metrically harmonious AABB rhyme scheme. Use a rhyming dictionary for assistance. Use exuberant language and expressive adjectives to evoke loving emotions stirred up by your dream.

Limerick

A limerick is a humorous, preposterous, suggestive or downright indecent ditty. It can be delightfully wacky, witty, nonsensical or bawdy. It is a playful rhyming form of poetry characterized by lighthearted clichés and puns with a rude or shocking punchline.

Try this!

Transpose an embarrassing, immoral, scurrilous or lascivious dream into the form of a limerick. Use a single-stanza verse of five lines with an AABBA rhyme scheme. The first, second and fifth lines should rhyme with eight or nine syllables each. The third and fourth lines should share a different rhyme and have five or six syllables each. Use a word-rhyming dictionary for a range of lyrics. Your limerick should be satirical with a sing-songy rhythm.

Pantoum

The pantoum poetry form is characterized by its repetitive style, which delves deeply into the emotions by building layers from recurring phrases. The strong repetition in a pantoum creates a circular web of thought, where the poem's final line is the same as its first, creating an echoing effect that shifts as the poem progresses.

Try this!

Extract the most emotionally charged phrases from your dream and use them as repetitive lines in varying sequences. The Pantoum form is composed of quatrains in which the second and fourth lines of the first stanza are repeated in the first and third lines of the next stanza. This pattern continues until the final stanza, where the opening line is repeated as the last line, creating a sense of closure.

Haiku

Haiku is an ancient Japanese poetic form that uses simple, sensory language to capture the essence of a single feeling, a brief point in time, a touching experience or an instant of satori. Typically, a haiku features a shift in mood or tone that leads to a moment of enlightenment and the revelation of a profound truth. A traditional Japanese Haiku is written with a strict form of three lines.

Try this!

Choose a poignant scene, idea or sentiment in your dream. Write three unrhymed lines composed of five syllables in the first line, seven syllables in the second line, and five syllables in the third line. Write with simplicity, clarity and directness of expression. Give your Haiku immediacy by using the present tense.

Ballad

Ballads are designed to narrate a tale in a sentimental, wistful, or sorrowful manner. Typically, ballads consist of slow, mellow verses that possess a melodic sing-song quality, capable of stirring intense feelings.

Try this!

Create a ballad that draws inspiration from a poignant dream and expresses the pain of a heart-wrenching relationship, a grave injustice or a sorrowful loss. Write your poem in four-line stanzas with a simple, melodic ABCB rhyme scheme. Use a rhyming dictionary to assist in the repetition of sounds. Repeat the first stanza as the last stanza.

Ditty

The ditty is a type of comic verse for children, using fun and silly rhymes. This poetic form is like a short, witty, finger-snapping jingle. It is a lighthearted, humorous approach to a simple single subject.

Dare to poke fun at one of your perplexing dream images. Choose an enigmatic situation, an out-of-place object or an annoying character as a thematic focus. Become snarky and churlish. Make your listeners snort with glee! Use a rhyming dictionary to make up some goofy rhymes.

Lampoon

A lampoon is a satire or a witty criticism that attacks broad social behaviors and vices through verse. It is exaggerated by dark humor and irony for comic effect.

Try this!

Create a parody that ridicules a dream through caricature, impersonation or imitation. Target flawed dream characters and mock them with exaggeration in a satiric way about their absurdity or irrelevancy. Write your poem in couplets with a delightfully provoking or wicked voice.

Found Poetry

By selecting titles and phrases from magazines and newspapers, it's possible to push the boundaries of a dream poem. The beauty of this approach is that you don't have to worry about writer's block or selecting the "perfect" words. Simply work with what you find. You can eliminate interference from your waking mind by letting go of preconceived interpretations and meanings of your dream.

Try this!

Select evocative words, descriptive lines and pithy phrases from magazine and newspaper headlines. Use these to craft a found-word poem that embraces the synchronicity of unexpected connections. You will rarely find exactly what you are looking for, so give up trying to control the process. Rather than trying to force a particular outcome, surrender yourself to what you find. Eliminate interference from your waking mind by and remain open to new poetic possibilities and insights.

3
DreamingArts

It does not suffice in all cases to elucidate only the conceptual context of a dream content. Often it is necessary to clarify a vague content by giving it a visible form. This can be done by drawing, painting, or modeling. Often the hands will solve a mystery that the intellect has struggled with in vain.

C.G. Jung

It is often difficult to fully express the visual elements of dreams using language alone. Given that dreams are frequently tricky to convert into words, deciphering them through word-centric journalling may seem an insurmountable task. To experience dreams in their own pictorial and imagistic language, it is helpful to engage in non-analytical, right-brain activities like the visual arts. DreamingArts activities, including painting, sketching, mapping, mask-making, and collage, provide diverse avenues to explore and express dreams.

Through DreamingArts activities, you can portray your dreams with your own primitive, hieroglyphic language, doodle with colorful crayons, cut out pictures from magazines, and scribble secrets in illegible codes with your non-dominant hand. By employing nonverbal techniques to express your dreams, you will establish neural pathways that bypass the logical part of the brain. The multi-sensory projects in the following section will assist you in describing the indescribable and expressing the inexplicable in your dreams.

Dreams and the Artist Within
Projects, Activities and Techniques to Spark Your Artistic Creativity

There is no art without intoxication. But I mean a mad intoxication! Let reason teeter! Delirium! The highest degree of delirium! Plunged in burning dementia! Art is the most enrapturing orgy within man's reach. Art must make you laugh a little and make you a little afraid.

Jean Dubuffet

In response to activities in this chapter, I have used one dream, "Molly Dog Returns," to demonstrate how a single dream can contain a multitude of varied interpretations. As you read through the following activities, you can toggle back and forth to compare each project here with its Molly Dream example in Part V.

Storyboard

A storyboard is a form of sequential storytelling. It is a visual medium for telling a story with pictures through a series of panels. A dream storyboard is a graphic representation of a nocturnal narrative that can be divided into separate scenes. It can serve as a helpful guide to navigate through a complicated dream journey.

Try this!

On an open page in your journal, divide the events from your dream into a collection of panels. Break down the actions and activities by mapping moments into bite-sized scenes. Use quick pencil sketches and stick figures in vignettes with simple borders. Use dialogue balloons for snippets of conversations. Draw arrows to illustrate the sequence of events and the passage of time.

Zoom In / Zoom Out

Exaggerating and reversing the scale of dream images can break the anxiety imposed by oppressive, antagonistic or annoying dreams. As a result of altering the interchange between overbearing and powerful dream images, we can diminish the weight they carry. When we let go of our attachment to the original version of a dream, we may be able to visualize a change in our waking life unions, connections, and alliances.

Try this!

Alter the vantage point from which you observe your dream images. Sketch out shifts in perspective by supersizing, minimizing, inflating, deflating, upscaling, and downscaling the relationships between characters or situations. Start by expanding the dominant forces while shrinking the weaker ones. Then reverse your viewpoint so that the weak are magnified and the powerful are diminished. When you alter the relationships between the dream images, pay attention to how it makes you feel when you apply the same turnabout to waking life relationships.

Mandala

A mandala is a form of sacred geometry used over the ages as a visual aid in active imagination meditation. As a personal development tool for harmony and psychic balance, it draws on ancient symbols used for magical, religious and shamanic purposes. These symbols are expressed in a configuration of concentric geometric shapes. The result is a microcosm of wholeness and completion.

Try this!

Reimagine your dream as a model of symmetry with circles, squares, crosses, triangles and spirals anchored around a central axis. Distill your dream images into simplified pictograms and design motifs. Repeat them in geometric rings as patterns of similarities, polarities, and intersections. By aligning your dream images into a mandala form, the apparent chaos of the dream narrative can be restructured into a unified whole where disparities and divisions join into a union of opposites.

Collage

Collage is an engrossing art form used by both artists and non-artists to illustrate a spontaneous response to dreams. Unlike other art forms that require training and expertise, collage is a calming and meditative practice suitable for all skill levels. The surprise of the found image is the key to collage. By discovering pictures and text in magazines, newspapers, and discarded books, dreams can take on a new light in unexpected ways. Collage demonstrates the magical power of synchronicity.

Try this!

With a sense of indulgent improvisation, your scissors and a glue stick in hand, excavate printed materials for evocative pictures from nature, art, architecture and science magazines that express the feelings provoked by a dream. Throw yourself at the mercy of the process of hunting and gathering. Be willing to stumble upon the unanticipated, the unpredictable and the unknown. You do not need to know where your dream collage will take you. Allow found images to play their tricks. Discover your aptitude for making fortunate discoveries accidentally. Trust that the evocative pictures you find will move your dreamwork forward. Listen to your heart and let go of the interference of your mind.

Dream Map

It is easy to feel lost when trying to find a way through a bewildering dream narrative. The actions in a dream often bring forth a host of entanglements, complications and convolutions. A visual map can help sort through complexities by rearranging dream symbols into diagrams. Mapping a dream can reveal correspondences, relationships and underlying patterns we might not otherwise see.

Try this!

Chart your dream story by mapping it out with simple figures and geometric shapes. Use circles, squares and triangles as symbols for characters, objects and obstacles. Use arrows to mark directions, waves to indicate actions and dotted lines to make connections. Add graphs and grids to show timelines. Use spirals to show where the dream action branches off in different directions. Mark ravines, drop-offs, dead ends, boundaries and borders between territories or emotional fields. Include alternative routes, shortcuts, bridges, escape hatches and the paths not taken.

Diorama

A diorama is a three-dimensional representation of a scene or setting in miniature with figures placed before a painted background inside a shoe box, a refurbished dollhouse or a shipping box turned on its side. A dream diorama stages a scene from a dream with tiny figurines, furniture, vehicles, flora and fauna placed throughout the container as a visual vignette.

Try this!

For your dream diorama, create a three-dimensional scene from simple materials inside a box or frame that is several inches deep. The container needs to have an open front so viewers can see inside. Paint a scene on the back of the container or create a collage from magazine cutouts to act as the background. Create figures with cardboard, modeling clay, styrofoam, pipe cleaners, popsicle sticks, found objects, aquarium plants and miniature toys. To place your figures, work from the back of the box toward the front, with smaller items placed in front of larger ones. Add layers of scenery to create depth. Glue everything down when you're satisfied with the arrangement.

Mask

Every night in dreams, we wear many masks and take on multiple identities. Mask-making has the power to alter our sense of self by transforming us into the likeness of the inhabitants of the dream world. Acting as a mediator between our waking persona and the beings of the nocturnal realm, a mask invites us to explore different dimensions of our inner selves. When we wear, move, and speak through a mask, we become a conduit between our singular waking persona and the denizens of the nighttime realm.

Try this!

Create a mask for one of your dream images. With hot glue, tape, scissors, felt and fabric scraps, fashion your mask from cardboard, a paper bag or a blank mask from a party store. For more dynamism, sculpt your mask with paper-mâché or mold a mask on your face with plaster gauze. Decorate your mask with paint, colored tissue, glitter, ribbons, feathers, bric-a-brac, baubles, bangles and beads. Attach an elastic band to keep it in place so you can wear it to enter the living experience of your dream through imaginal play.

Painting

Painting is a sensuous experience that taps into the raw emotions of the soul. Dream Painting captures feelings and articulates sensations. Spontaneous gestures portray spatial and nonverbal concepts that bypass the cognitive processes of speech and language. Without yielding to the pressures of formal composition, the process liberates us from rules and expectations. Dream painting is not about talent, aptitude, or achievement. It enables a deep connection and direct experience with dreams, unlocking potent energy fields that can lead to profound insights.

Try this!

Animate your dream's vitality and spirit with your brush and a pallet of paint. Even if you don't consider yourself an artist, try splashing around with lyrical swirls of paint to convey the feelings in the dream. Let paint flow over and around your journal pages, sketchbook or canvas. Invite colors to move and merge in and around each other. Let the texture of the paint be beautiful, awkward or chaotic. Play in a non-linear, non-logical, undisciplined manner with the looseness of a child. Focus on the energy fields and abstract currents that emanate from the dream. Let yourself scribble, smear, slather and splatter paint without judgment or critical evaluation. Give way to spontaneous, expansive expression. Take risks. Let the unexpected unfold. Allow the process to surprise you.

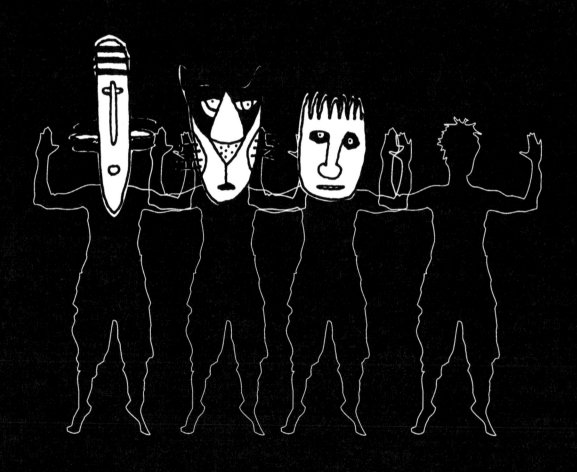

4
Dream Theater

The great joy of play, fantasy and the imagination is that for a time, we are utterly spontaneous, free to imagine anything. In such a pure state of pure being, no thought is unthinkable.

C.G. Jung

Acting out dreams is a playful, interactive approach rather than an analytic one. As such, it can circumvent some of the cerebral intellectualizing that accompanies dream work. Incorporating role-playing, either alone or in collaboration with a dream group, can enhance the authenticity of dream narratives. Rather than interpreting a dream, a theatrical portrayal allows the dream to be mirrored and experienced through monologues, dialogues, songs, screenplays and impromptu performances. The theater arts techniques presented in the following section can help you create powerful and revealing dramatizations and comedic re-enactments of your dreams by forging a strong connection between your dream life and waking life. (See the section titled "Guidelines for Dream Groups.")

Dreams and the Thespian Within

Projects, Activities and Techniques to Animate Your Imaginative Play

Pretending is not just play. Pretending is imagined possibility.

Meryl Streep

In response to activities in this chapter, I have used one dream, "Molly Dog Returns," to demonstrate how a single dream can contain a multitude of varied interpretations. As you read through the following activities, you can toggle back and forth to compare each project here with its Molly Dream example in Part V.

Monologue

In a theatrical production, monologues provide an opportunity for characters to reveal their innermost thoughts and emotions regarding the events unfolding around them. Through stage whispers and confidential remarks, characters share their unique perspectives with the audience, providing valuable insights into their motivations. These asides offer valuable character's intentions, obsessions, and secret desires while featuring their triumphs and disappointments.

Try this!

Compose and perform a monologue from the viewpoint of one of your dream characters. Adopt a persona that is innocent, infantile; self-righteous, cynical, egotistical, eccentric, or psychotic. Express the inner thoughts that your character feels compelled to share. When addressing your dream group, remain in character and use the first person, present tense.

Dialogue

In a play, the characters' interactions with each other can reveal much about their personalities. The dialogue they share is a powerful tool for developing their connection, whether it's through arguments, expressions of love, or the sharing of important news. By engaging in dialogue, dream characters can reveal their innermost fears, deep-seated desires, virtues, vices, strengths, and weaknesses. As they interact, their sentiments towards one another are gradually unveiled.

Try this!

Compose and perform a character sketch between two dream beings from an emotionally charged dream. Use two distinct voices, differing speech patterns and contrasting tones. Flesh out each character with different moods and styles; seductive, melodious, domineering, deceitful or foolish. Set up a conflict in which one character strikes terror while the other is frightened; one manipulates while the other acquiesces; one accuses while the other defends; one woos while the other demurs. Create the kind of meaty, challenging roles actors love.

Campfire Story

Campfire tales are traditionally spun in the dark of night with intensity, mystery and suspense. They feature larger-than-life villains and impossible challenges told with exaggerations and embellishments. They provoke and arouse the emotions with a twisted life lesson at the end. Transforming a nightmare into a vivid campfire potboiler can be empowering for a dreamer by mocking nocturnal torments and fears.

Try this!

Turn your dream into a chilling ghost story or an exaggerated tall tale to share with your dream group, as if you were gathered around a campfire. Choose a dream with a quirky plot line, irrational fear or spooky characters. Dramatize all the parts as you refashion the dream with suspense, surprise, hilarity and delight. Mime different postures and movements for each character. Use bold gestures and strong body language. Stand up, sit down, move around, and make eye contact while you tell your tale. Change voices, speak in different accents, change your volume, pitch and pace. Punctuate your dialog with squeals, squawks, snorts and sighs. Mimic facial expressions as you squint, stare or sneer. When the story gets to the really, really scary part, let your voice get softer. Take dramatic pauses. Become a raconteur, a spinner of yarns. Invite your dream group to respond with cheers, hisses and boos with sound effects by banging pots, blowing whistles, hooting and clapping. Give your tale a preposterous or corny ending. Consider incorporating a pun or play on words into the final line for added humor.

Screenplay

A screenplay lays the groundwork for a film or stage production, detailing its characters, actions, dialogue, movement, and stage directions. It is written in concise, declarative sentences in the present tense. The story usually involves the main character facing various challenges and encountering victories and defeats. In most screenplays, the pinnacle moment is when the hero and villain confront each other.

Try this!

Select a dream that creates empathy through actions the audience can see and dialogue the audience can hear. Begin each scene with a clear location and time of day, and list the cast of characters involved. Identify the protagonist and antagonist, and consider both external and internal challenges for each character. Use dialogue to craft emotionally dynamic interactions. Establish clear stage directions with transitions that fade in and out between scenes. Show, don't tell.

Song

Music has the ability to communicate feelings and ideas by combining poetic lyrics with rhythmic patterns. The melody of a song has the power to evoke the energy and vitality of a dream through harmony, tone, and rhythm. Songs can evoke sentimental crescendos of extravagant tenderness, irreconcilable differences, or soulful sorrows.

Try this!

Select a favorite tune to express the emotional timbre of your dream. Find a golden oldie, folk song, familiar lullaby or beloved aria to fit your dream story. Write, alter or steal original lyrics to help you rhapsodize the joy and pathos in your dream. Use a rhyming dictionary to shape your vocals into soulful ballads or romantic serenades. Sing your song for your dream group.

Melodrama

A melodrama is a humorous allegory with an improbable plot and stereotypical characters. The story always concerns the vicissitudes suffered by the virtuous at the hands of the villainous. Good-vs-Evil morality tales inevitably involve a perilous dilemma or impending danger in which hyperbole makes mountains out of molehills and mincemeat out of monsters. The theatrics always end happily with virtue triumphant. Melodramas use themes of mistaken identities, unrequited love, romantic triangles, greed, lust, foul play, revenge and chaos. Humor and mayhem can help defuse an extremely tense, hostile or volatile dream. Melodrama can turn the terror of onerous dream incidents into foolish pranks and harmless threats.

Try this!

Take a thorny dream and reinvent it by rewriting it as a melodrama. Meddle with your notion of the dream. Refuse to take it seriously. Make a travesty of primal fears and make a fool of the offenders. Give way to gross desires and larger-than-life passions. Allow dream images to undermine the pretensions of your ego with taunting voices that deflate your fundamental beliefs and belittle your values. Taunt the terrible. Mock the morbific. Ridicule the nature of disturbing dream beings with idiotic babbling and buffoonery. Expose secrets and repressed feelings. Skoff at moments of vanity and ambition. Dare to be impetuous and reckless.

Body and Soul

Words and pictures alone cannot express the dynamic nature of dreams. Improvisational, body-based rhythms can connect the sensations of a dream in a passionate, nonverbal way. Free-flowing motions, gestures and body language can tap into vast reservoirs of emotional depth. Through spontaneous movement, the energy fields of dreams become activated. Their innate vitality releases kinetic energy. By sending dream images pulsing, pumping and circulating throughout your waking body, the boundaries between the self and the "other" dissolve.

Try this!

Find a place to move about freely. Choose musical accompaniment with a beat or melody that suits the tempo and mood of your dream. Animate and mimic one of your dream entities through rhythmic movement and breath. Feel what it's like to embody a being of the night. Become energetically involved with your dream being so its heart beats in your heart, its blood flows through your veins, and its feelings burn within you. Feel how your physical framework changes shape and size as you take different positions and postures. Flex and stretch, leap and fall, twirl and shake. There is no need to interpret the movements; simply experience them. Even slight gestures and subtle micro-movements can animate the dream body. Invite each dream image to move you and to move through you. Become a shapeshifter.

Stage the Dream

DreamTheater is a full-immersion, interactive experience that brings a dream to life and fosters a powerful, synergistic connection within a dream group. It invites participants to collaborate together, collectively experiencing a dream narrative chosen by one of the dream group members. Serving as the director, the dreamer can play their own part or assign someone else to portray their role. The setting can be assembled from chairs and tables rearranged in the room. Everyday objects can be used as props. Costumes can be as simple as a box full of colorful scarves. Unlike passive methods of dream interpretation, DreamTheater's physicality offers a direct and unfiltered experience of the dream, free from the influence of analytical thinking.

To create your dream play, assign various roles to members of your dream group. As the director, guide your cast in delivering their lines, coordinating their actions, and providing them with essential cues. Make recommendations and corrections as you rehearse, but also be open to improvised movements and body language by the players. Extra group members can function as a chorus to echo important lines and provide sound effects. If the dream lacks a conclusion, the cast can experiment with different endings and resolutions. After blocking it out, perform the dream. Play your role or watch from the wings as your dream story unfolds. After the play has been performed, initiate a discussion with your dream group to exchange insights and revelations.

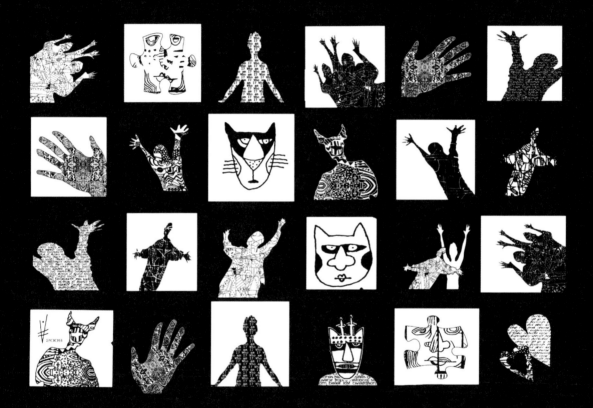

5
DreamJourneys

If we truly want to know the secret of soulful travel, we need to believe that there is something sacred waiting to be discovered in virtually every journey.

Phil Cousineau

The upcoming section features experiential projects intended to reorganize complex dreams through imaginative mind games. They are filled with creative approaches to establish new connections between the inner and the outer mind. Acting as springboards to traverse the imaginal world through time and space, the following projects dig into deep dream ecology, where you will be invited to take risks and to make extraordinary leaps of faith. By engaging in these projects, you will uncover new layers of understanding while playfully ambushing your powers of rational reasoning.

Dreams and the Explorer Within

Projects, Activities and Techniques to Stimulate Your Imagination

Leap and the net will appear.

Maurice Sendak

 In response to activities in this chapter, I have used one dream, "Molly Dog Returns," to demonstrate how a single dream can contain a multitude of varied interpretations. As you read through the following activities, you can toggle back and forth to compare each project here with its Molly Dream example in Part V.

Fairy Tale

Fairy tales are fanciful, highly improbable accounts of heroic characters, legendary deeds, magical creatures, cautionary plots and moralistic outcomes. Handed down from generation to generation across many different world cultures, they feature universal motifs and common elements in which the ending must resolve conflicts and show a moral transformation. Dreams are similar to fairy tales. Both feature fantastic stories that require a suspension of reality as we know it. Both are filled with archetypal characters in symbolic narratives where anything is possible. Both offer psychological and spiritual insights.

Try this!

Transpose your dream into a fairy tale. Reimagine your dreamscape as an enchanted place where everything is animated and alive. Transform your dream beings into classic fairy tale characters: heroes, villains, wizards, witches, kings, queens, knights, fools, paupers, hags, misers, minstrels and monsters. Imbue inanimate dream objects with speech or magical powers. Use exaggeration to make small dream images very, very small and large images very, very large. Use traditional fairy tale adjectives, absolutes, superlatives and clichés to hyperbolize the emotions in your dream. Cast magical spells, charms, hexes, curses, enchantments and incantations to advance the plot. Fill your tale with invocations, prohibitions, passwords, warnings, secrets, curses and omens. Invent improbable plot twists. Fabricate inflated dialogue. Add magical interventions, secret knowledge or ancient wisdom from a Wise One to help resolve conflicts. Create a fable-like title for your dream. Set it in the past tense in a distant time when the world was rife with magic. Begin with Once Upon a Time…. End your tale with a moral or a lesson to be learned.

Board Game

Similar to the world of board games, dreams often navigate through territories of dark and light in a checkered journey where the conscious vies with the unconscious in fundamental archetypal conflicts. Board games reflect universal patterns of life in which players compete in a miniature landscape striving to overcome odds, gain control over conflicting forces, master the rules and outwit opponents. Traditional games require skill and talent, but in most games, players are subject to the unpredictable elements of chance as well. Players never know what the next card, move or roll of the dice will hold. With the luck of the draw, they might win or lose everything.

Try this!

Turn your dream into a game. Design a game board that mirrors the landscape or environment of your dream. Select character tokens representing dream beings, animals or objects for playing pieces. Designate a starting point called "Home," and determine the number of players. Decide how the playing pieces will move across the board. In your dream game, players may compete for wealth, property, or survival, as they navigate through a maze of shortcuts and setbacks. The gameplay may be determined by cards or dice, causing players to bump, slide, advance, return, or be sent back home. Players might jump forward with wild cards or be thrown on the discard pile with jokers. Compile a rule book with instructions on how to play your dream game. What is the name of the game? What is the goal? What are the obstacles? What are the penalties and rewards? What strategies, tools or tactics are required to play? Who are the opponents? Do they need to be eliminated? When does the dream game end? How is the game won?

Comic Strip

Comic strips are a unique way of telling a story through visual art, using drawings to create a humorous narrative. Exaggeration and shifting points of view in comic style can add razzmatazz to the unfolding of dream scenarios. Opting for a whimsical approach can provide a satirical take on a dream that might otherwise seem intimidating.

Copy clipart from the internet to portray characters and scenes from your dream story. Use emoticons, glyphs, spirals, zig-zags, stars, hearts, squiggly lines and dots to express action and emotional charge. Use captions, thought bubbles and dialogue balloons for punchy lines. Play with fonts to add expressive sound effects and punctuation, such as Whoosh! Boom! Kapow! Splot! Squish! Ping! Pow! Shazaam! Vroom! Bam! Whaam! Uggg! Ha Ha!, Whuh? #@*%$&!

Alice in Dreamland

Burning with curiosity, Alice follows the White Rabbit into a strange and curious wonderland. She travels through a lopsided world that doesn't obey logical rules. Alice wonders if she has changed in the night. If she is not who she was, who in the world is she? Alice converses with herself as she tries to make sense of this bizarre, upside-down, inside-out dream world. She has conversations with strange characters, animals and entities she meets along her journey. Although she tries very hard to remain sane and logical, she is often misunderstood and confronted by irritable creatures who pose riddles and make unreasonable demands. They make rude remarks and ask impossible questions that Alice can't answer. Alice doesn't like being confronted and criticized, so she begins asking the questions.

Try this!

Invite Alice to fall into your dream and wander as an impartial observer through your dreamscape. What people, animals and dream events does Alice find peculiar, odd or absurd? Encourage her to engage with your dream inhabitants through respectful, innocent inquiry and curiosity. Take note of the logical questions she might pose and imagine how the beings of your dreams might respond. Record the questions and answers which may or may not make sense.

Mythic Journey

Peering into our dreams through a mythic lens, we can explore the ancient wisdom embedded in our nocturnal meanderings. Like mythic encounters, dreams often unfold with archetypal forces that ask us to see our lives as sacred, spiritual quests. Dreams can catapult us into a dimension far beyond our daily lives.

Transform a dream into a legendary adventure by changing your characters into gods, goddesses, demons, heroes, and mortals. Begin your tale with a divine calling or initiation. Develop your narrative around a mythic theme of temptation, a risk, a loss of innocence, a test of courage or a surrender. Conclude your myth with a confrontation of a dragon of fear, a noble sacrifice, a heart-breaking defeat, a triumphant accomplishment, or a discovery of a priceless treasure. Set your tale in the past tense as if it has been passed down throughout the ages from a distant time and place.

Child's Play

It is common for dreams to evoke memories from childhood. Our past homes, schools, and events can become intertwined with our current dream stories as we see old acquaintances and long-lost relatives mixed with our present family members, coworkers, and friends. Amalgamated in bizarre combinations, themes of youthful identity and dependence may bring up present feelings of guilt, shame, doubt, or confusion around gender.

Try this!

Select a dream that brings back memories, sensations, activities, and emotions from your childhood. Become one with your vulnerable, trusting, and curious inner child. Invite your younger self to speak freely with the forgotten voice of your tender, innocent years.

Honor Bound

When we ignore our personal values and adhere instead to societal norms, familial expectations, or religious dogmas, our dreams often compromise our integrity. This can lead to unsettling nightmares where we become prey to negative entities and feelings of guilt and self-doubt. By swapping perspectives with different dream characters, we can see into the mirror of our self-betrayal.

Try this!

Sketch a series of vignettes to release yourself from condemnation and domination. Untie the knots of self-criticism with self-respect. Release all liability and responsibility for being judgmental. Refuse to let negative images do your thinking and talking. Let your authentic self shine through. Elevate your dignity. You have the power to change your story.

Portrait of Power

Dreams often involve intense struggles for power, with dictatorial characters ruling the night. As a result, dreamers may wake up feeling helpless, their aspirations muted, and their objectives thwarted. However, by exploring challenging dreams using found text and images, dreamers may uncover unexpected revelations that empower them to confront their difficult dreams with newfound personal strength.

Collage a series of tableaux in your journal that reflect themes of power and powerlessness from a tyrannical dream. Superimpose expressive words and clippings from the newspaper over evocative pictures and photographs from magazines. Let the synchronicity of found imagery and text surprise you with new connections to the oppressive events in your dream.

Describe the power dynamics depicted in your collages. Which images appear dominant, overwhelming, or invincible? Conversely, which images seem weak, defenseless or unsafe? Describe your emotional reaction to the depictions of both repression and emancipation in your artwork. Have you relinquished your power, or have you claimed it for yourself?

Pandora's Dream Box

Pandora, a mythical figure, was initially an earth goddess. The gods transformed her into a mortal woman graced with irresistible charm and an insatiable curiosity. They entrusted her with a jar containing the evils of humanity, warning her never to open it. However, as her story is commonly told, Pandora's inquisitive nature led her to open the jar, releasing all the wickedness within to plague the world. The term "Pandora's Box" now refers to a container holding all things mischievous, immoral, and subversive. This cautionary tale is intended to thwart our innate desire to explore the unknown as it may lead us to confront the hidden, darker parts of ourselves. Yet, knowledge of the shadow side is essential for unleashing profound insights in dream work. The retelling of the Pandora myth often neglects to mention that "Hope" remained inside the jar. Like the Hope in Pandora's Box, there is always a gift of healing and wholeness inside the shadows of even the most challenging dream.

Try this!

Use a thesaurus to create a list of synonyms for the negative expressions in your dream. Print the negative vocabulary words onto paper strips, curl them with the edge of a knife and stuff them in a box. To counter your collection of negative words, use an antonym dictionary to find a range of positive expressions from your dream. Write words of positivity onto strips of paper, curl them with the edge of a knife and glue them to the interior roof of the box. Close the box.

    Take a few deep meditative breaths and create a ceremonial moment. Light a candle, ring a bell. Focus on your dream. Take the lid off your box. Spill all the negative words out so that only the positive words are left bonded to the cover. Release all the negativity that has been boxed up inside so it is no longer trapped in your psyche. Consider how the hope-filled words of positivity can sustain you and support you. Close the container, keeping only the positive words inside. Open your Pandora's box before bedtime and read your words to incubate a healing dream.

Pearl of Great Price

A pearl is formed when a foreign particle or parasite invades the delicate inner flesh of an oyster. As a means of self-protection against this irritant, the oyster shell deposits layers of Mother of Pearl. Remarkably, this defensive process produces a rare, lustrous gemstone. The protection that turns pain and suffering into a jewel of incomparable beauty has become an esoteric metaphor for healing wisdom known as "The Pearl of Great Price."

Try this!

In your journal, riff about an aggravating irritant within an annoying dream. Notice how this bothersome dream image has gotten under your skin. Ruminate about how you have traditionally defended yourself from this invasive feeling. Imagine a way to turn the affliction in your dream into a treasure of great value. Invoke the Mother of Pearl. Petition her for guidance, support and a sense of ease, serenity, and tranquility. Ask her to help you turn your irritation into a pearl of wisdom.

Witches' Brew

The most noxious of dream narratives can be calmed by conjuring up a magical potion of protection from the painful effects of unsettling dreams. The hangover residue from nightmares can be overpowered by "cooking up" a hell-broth of socially inappropriate behaviors and attitudes. Once the brew has been concocted from malice and moral outrage, the toxins can be transformed into a curative elixir. Nighttime perturbations can be cast off, expunged and banished by invoking the imaginal powers of witchery.

Try this!

Create a witches' brew from the ingredients of a dark dream. Mix up a combination of paralyzing anxieties, trepidations and consternations in a large cauldron of words. Thicken your potion with undisciplined fantasies, outrageous desires and untamed emotions. Bring your brew to a literary boil with the potent power of your imagination. Take a sip. Then, get the bitter taste out of your system by scribbling preventative incantations, protective hexes and restorative enchantments. Call forth your inner witch to cast a spell against your horrible dream so it will never again torment you.

A New Ending

When we dream, we often find ourselves wandering in search of something elusive, something that has been lost, someone who has disappeared, a question unanswered, a problem unsolved. We awaken, yearning for something beyond the edge of what we dreamed or can remember. One way to achieve a feeling of closure is to re-enter the dream space to alter the storyline by completing an unfinished dream, resolving a predicament, or inventing a new ending.

Try this!

Find an unresolved issue in your dream. Use active imagination to carry the dream narrative forward. Modify, alter and revise your dream. If you failed to act in the dream, write about taking action. If some predicament is undecided, invent a resolution. If there is someone you didn't confront, challenge them. If something is blocking your path, extricate yourself. If a sense of helplessness diminishes you, call forth your power. Let unexpected things happen. Be blatantly inventive. Don't concern yourself with plausibility. Let your imagination take wing. Transform delusions into illuminations. Change directions, go past impassable barriers. Confront your fears. Invent solutions and resolutions. Write a new ending.

Labyrinth

A labyrinth is a meandering unicursal path that winds its way towards a central point and back out again. It is often used for meditation during ritual and ceremony, as well as for personal, psychological, and spiritual transformation. Walking through the serpentine paths of a labyrinth can be beneficial when reflecting on the intricate nature of a recurring dream. Despite its apparent complexity, there is a hidden unity and order within .

Try this!

Immerse yourself in the power of a labyrinth by visiting one located in a church, garden, park, or spiritual sanctuary. As you approach the entrance, take a deep breath and turn your attention inward. Concentrate on a recurring theme that repeats in your dreams. Once inside, allow yourself to become fully present with the sensations and emotions that arise within you. As you navigate the twists and turns of the labyrinth, challenge your assumptions about how the patterns in your dreams reflect those in your waking life. Like your dream life, your waking life is a journey of constant change and growth. With each change in direction, the switchbacks on the path are a reminder that in every end, there is a new beginning. By walking a labyrinth, you can re-experience the opposing inner forces of the night and merge them into a cohesive reflection of your outer life.

Sanctuary

When we encounter challenging dreams, we often tend to fixate on the most distressing elements and overlook the less troubling details. However, similar to the stillness in the eye of a hurricane, challenging dreams often have a moment of tranquility within them which can be discovered if we are willing to seek it out. Reflecting on a calm, gentle dream detail can release the grip of a nightmare and bring a sense of peacefulness to the soul.

Try this!

To find inner peace within a disturbing dream, search for a moment of serenity. Imagine a place of safety or a hiding place where you can feel balanced, calm and out of harm's way. Envision a shelter with a clear boundary where you cannot be accused, refused or pursued. If there is no safe space in your dream, conjure up an imaginary place of refuge. Create a sacred ground within your dreaming soul that you can trust utterly.

Utopian Vision

Our dreams often take us out of our comfort zones and challenge our sense of honor, righteousness and respectability. We may feel like unknown forces are pushing and pulling us, leaving us with no control over the dilemmas that arise. But what if we alter the provocations of our dreams? What if we dare to turn our worst dreams into our best dreams? DreamJourneys invite us to use our imagination to replace fear with courage, anger with tranquility, loathing with respect, cruelty with kindness, and blame with forgiveness. Through our powers of invention, we can envision another way of being in both the dream world and in the waking world.

Try this!

Turn a disturbing dream around by inverting unsettling feelings with a change of vocabulary. Consult an antonym dictionary to find words that are opposite to your dream's negative expressions. Rewrite your dream by turning every dark dream image to light. Reverse each negative emotion with soothing words of confidence, comfort and safety. Recreate the ending of your dream so that you and all of your dream beings triumph, prosper and thrive. Nothing changes in the waking world that hasn't been envisioned in the imagination first.

Prayer

When we pray, we express our innermost desires and longings to a divine entity or higher power. Personal prayer can be a plea for absolution, a request for peace, or a fervent appeal for healing. A dream prayer can turn a personal dream meditation into a universal experience connecting with all humanity through the collective unconscious.

Try this!

Compose a prayer to ease the emotional distress you experience in a difficult dream. Ask for divine intervention to calm your inner turmoil. Offer a heartfelt plea for all people everywhere who suffer in the night. Beseech your divine presence to replace the turbulence in nightmarish dreams with universal peace, love and compassion for all living souls.

Guidelines For Dream Groups

*The real voyage of discovery lies not in finding new lands
but in seeing with fresh eyes.*

Marcel Proust

The DreamingArts practice can be a lonely undertaking. You might find yourself challenged when embarking on this path by yourself. Starting or joining a dream group can offer significant advantages. As you move through the projects and exercises in this book, a group of curious and respectful fellow dreamers can help you learn the language of dreams by collaborating with you as imaginative detectives.

Dreams are mostly visual experiences, which can easily deceive dreamers with the optical illusions created by their surface appearance. Fellow dreamers hear a spoken version. They are not bound to take the dream literally. They can hear slips of the tongue, puns, idiomatic expressions, double entendres, and unconscious inferences that the dreamer doesn't notice. Sharing a dream within a respectful and curious environment often leads to a shift in frames of reference. With multiple points of view from varied perspectives, group dreamwork can uncover illuminations and revelations that may not have been discovered by the individual dreamer alone. Dreamers with diverse

backgrounds can provide valuable insights from their life experiences as well as their understanding of archetypal motifs, depth psychology, mythology, literature, history, religion, and science. The combined intelligence of a group of like-minded seekers can unravel the multi-dimensional worlds of paradox, allegory and metaphor in intuitive ways.

Dreams are unique to each individual. They can differ greatly in theme and content. Some people dream in vibrant colors, while others see their dreams in black and white. Some may have ordinary dreams about mundane tasks, while others embark on epic journeys. Some may only dream in fragments, while others spin elliptical narratives with confusing twists and turns. It is important to remember that every dream is a personal creation, and no dream should be judged based on its length or complexity. All dreams have great depth, and all dreams are welcome.

Curiosity is the simplest, most direct way to talk about a dream. If the dreamer invites discussion, an excellent place to start is with clarifying questions. Fellow dreamers should maintain an attitude of inquisitiveness and not be in a rush to interpret or analyze. Questions may be more potent than answers. Participants should avoid leading questions and putting words in the dreamer's mouth. Dream group members don't have to study Sigmund Freud and Carl Jung or hold a PhD in depth psychology to offer valuable insights. The big trick of effective dream-sharing is to stay in the place of "not-knowing."

Once the group has opened up a dream with questions, the dreamer may invite suggestions from the group. It is important to remember that comments made by group

members are only projections of their own experiences and feelings. DreamWorker Jeremy Taylor suggests it is respectful to offer opinions in the first person, carefully following a phrase like "In my imagined version of the dream…". By phrasing opinions this way, the dreamer can accept or reject suggestions.

Listening to a dream is comparable to hearing the plot of a motion picture in a few minutes. Dream group participants visualize the dream from a spoken or sketched account, which differs from how the dreamer experienced it. What the dreamer sees clearly, the listener/observer has to imagine. Many details get left out. No one but the dreamer knows what the dream characters and dreamscapes actually look like or how the actions impact the emotions underlying the telling of the tale. For each dream told, multiple versions will be envisioned in the room. The meaning and emotional content of the dream may differ for each member of the group.

When forming a dream group, ensure that all participants agree to a commitment of total focus in an uninterrupted time frame. The group is responsible for paying full attention to the dreamer's narration without interruption or judgment and with complete confidentiality. Exchanging dreams can foster a rich camaraderie among partners, siblings, relatives, colleagues, caregivers, spiritual seekers and friends. However, it's important to note that dreamwork can uncover unexpected revelations. When sharing dreams, you are revealing a deeply personal and sensitive part of your being. Memories will be triggered, and emotions will rise. Do not share dreams with anyone who might push your buttons or betray your confidence. Dream sharing is not a parlor game. Make sure that all participants understand the limits and boundaries of respectful dreamwork. (See the IASD Ethics Statement in Appendix A)

During the process of sharing dreams, the dreamer holds the ultimate authority and has the power to cease or alter the conversation's direction at any point. Even if fellow group members believe they understand the dream's content, they must respect the dreamer's right to accept or reject any interpretation offered. Each dreamer should be given the time and space to uncover the meaning of their dream at their own pace. The true significance of dream imagery lies in the emotional resonance that the dreamer feels, and only they can confidently determine what the dream represents. This realization often comes through an intuitive, wordless Aha! This is the moment of recognition when the dream has revealed a profound personal truth.

The projects in this book can serve as a soul-centered study guide for an ongoing or emerging dream group. By engaging in creative improvisations with like-minded individuals, the door to the mysteries of existence will open with the magic, awe and grace.

Dream Group Invocation

Creating a group ceremony is a respectful way to shift gears from the waking world. Mark the beginning of your group session with a blessing by lighting a candle, ringing a bell, reading a poem or offering a prayer. Call in the spirits of the dreamtime.

May our stories of the night inspire us
to use our intuition, our power and our delight;
To sing the songs
of our loves, our sorrows, our light and our losses;
To heal, to bless, to create;
To reveal the gifts of the spirit of the dreams
within us.

Shekhinah,
We praise you who dwells in our midst
as Mother, Mentor and Muse.
In praising you,
we acknowledge that all dreams are sacred.
With every dream light we kindle,
the world is brightened to a higher harmony.

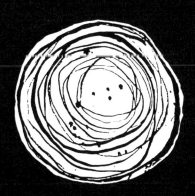

*In the middle of the journey of my life I came to myself
within a dark wood where the straight way was lost.*
        Dante Alighieri

PART V
THE ART OF ONE DREAM

A DREAM of MY DOG, MOLLY:
A DreamingArts Case Study

In this chapter, I use one dream to illustrate all fifty-five DreamingArts activities and techniques offered in the previous chapters. The Molly Dream, which I titled "Molly Dog Returns," is a dream that represents the profound breadth and depth that one dream can hold. It is a short, simple dream that I hope you, the reader, will feel some kinship with. Although this dream bears the markings of my own distinctive hallmark, I believe it also has the imprint of universal themes that will speak to you. It touches on predominant, deep-rooted motifs: loss of love, abuse in the name of love, and love at its transcendent, unconditional apex. Through fifty-five DreamingArts activities, I hope to demonstrate how a single dream can hold multiple levels of significance and change the direction of a life.

Molly Dog Returns

My beloved dog Molly is alive again! She has returned to my home. She appears much bigger, more beautiful and hairier than she was in life. She has been hanging out with my husband and me upstairs in the living room, but she has left her droppings downstairs in my art studio!

Upstairs, I hear an angry voice on the radio screaming and hollering at a dog... Somehow I know my husband has been scolding Molly for pooping on my studio floor. I confront him. He admits that he has been yelling at Molly. He has been feeding her along with the cats, so he feels entitled to discipline her.

For the first time in our marriage, I stand up to him. I tell him he is not to yell at my Molly ever again. From now on, I will feed her and take care of her.

I think the matter is settled, but the following morning, I hear the same radio program repeating the angry voice over and over... And I know that my husband has ignored me and is hollering at Molly again.

Molly Dream Lexicon

Journal Notes from My Life Log
Recent Life Events, Connections, Associations, Insights

The day before this dream, my computer "dropped" the course outline for my approaching dream workshop. The project document I had spent so much time tweaking and streamlining simply vanished from the computer. I sat at my desk downstairs, facing my computer in disbelief, uncharacteristically foaming oaths and expletives at the top of my lungs.

My husband heard me and came downstairs to my studio. He was always willing to be helpful, so he offered to look at what went wrong. But when he couldn't find the missing document, he blamed me for its loss, saying I must have done something wrong. We had our usual tussle. He repeated over and over and over the steps I had already taken to recover the file. He accused me of causing the problem. I had less than one hour to prepare new notes for my workshop, but my husband was still seated at my computer, treating me like an imbecile, looping over and over, ranting and blaming me for what I did wrong. I became so exasperated that I blew up.

Confrontation is not in my nature, but there was no other way to stop his obsessive blame game. I pushed him out of my office, screaming, I can't deal with your explosive anger any longer! I wanted him to experience how it feels to be yelled at. I had taken enough of his rage, his tirades and his pattern of shaming and blaming. But I never knew how to stop him from yelling at me. So I started copying his behavior. My husband was genuinely shocked. He did not realize that I was mirroring his volatile behavior. He just didn't get my message.

Dream Characters

List each character that appears in the dream.

HUSBAND:

A Husband is a male partner entrusted to love, honor, and obey, 'till death do us part.

My Husband is my chosen life partner. He intrigues me with his brilliance and talent. He is also a computer wiz. I am so grateful to have a techie husband to set up and maintain my laptop. Whenever I have technical difficulties, he always stops what he is doing and comes to my aid. But his offer of help often winds up with habitual, automatic anger and blame if he can't fix the problem (as it did the day before I had this dream.) He feels free to rant and rave whenever he gets upset, and he gets upset a lot. I always make excuses for his outbursts, knowing he had an abusive childhood. I repeat to myself that he can't help himself.

In my dream, he repeatedly yells at my dog, Molly. But in waking life, he never yelled at her. He loved her.

THE ANGRY VOICE ON THE RADIO:

In my dream, I hear a disembodied, unknown, unseen male voice ranting and raging on the airwaves. The voice is scolding, rebuking and criticizing a dog.

It sounds like the voices of all the men in my life: my father would holler with abusive outbursts; my brother would scream and bully; my husband would rage.

The voice also sounds like the angry men on authoritarian news programs broadcasting misogynistic messages throughout the world.

ME:

I am an artist, writer, and teacher of dreams. I have a spacious studio in which I create multi-media artworks, write my books and host seminars and workshops. I think of myself as easygoing. I avoid conflict. I tend to keep my anger inside.

I am a wife, a sister and a daughter to men who get angry and yell. I have always been afraid to confront these angry men since their temper tends to escalate quickly, leaving me vulnerable and defenseless.

In my dream, I am delighted to be reunited with my dog Molly. I confront my angry husband for yelling, but he continues to ignore me even after I finally speak up.

Dream Creatures

List the animals in the dream.

DOG:

A dog is a domesticated animal, trained to be well-behaved. It needs love and attention. It needs to be walked, fed, groomed, and protected. A dog is a faithful companion whose love is unconditional. A dog is eager to please. It takes a lot to break a dog's spirit. To treat someone like a dog is to mistreat them. To dog someone is to judge or criticize them.

In mythology, a dog is often a Psychopomp—a spirit guide, a mediator between the living and the dead.

MOLLY:

Molly was my big, shaggy, dear doggie. She has been dead for many years. She was my loving, faithful companion. She was always by my side. We were a team. She loved me unconditionally. I have never been loved by anyone the way Molly loved me.

In my dream, Molly has returned home even though she has been dead in the waking world for years. In my dream, I know she is alive and living at home, but her presence is implied by the droppings left downstairs in my studio. She doesn't actually appear! Yet, she is the intermediary that sets up the action between my husband and me.

CATS:

Cats are aloof, detached and impervious to angry voices. No one can bend their will or change their behavior. They are oblivious to criticism or reproach. Scolding them doesn't affect them at all.

In my dream, my husband has been feeding Molly along with our cats. They are merely mentioned and not a part of the action in the dream at all.

Dream Objects

List the inanimate objects in the dream.

THE RADIO:

A radio is a device for broadcasting communications. It receives signals and transmits messages. A radio has to be plugged into the house current. It has a dial that controls the volume and a switch that can be turned on or off.

In my dream, the radio is tuned to a channel broadcasting a threatening, menacing voice. It repeats the same program over and over in a series of repetitive loops. This radio is sending a negative signal throughout my home.

THE DROPPINGS:

Droppings are made of excrement. If a pet eliminates its feces on an indoor floor, the droppings are often unpleasant, disgraceful, nasty and filthy.

I think of all the toxic shit in my home life I don't want to deal with.

The day before my dream, My computer *dropped* my Word document, which led my husband to offer his help. But when he couldn't fix the problem, he exploded. On that day, the bottom of our marriage *dropped* out.

In my dream, Molly has *dropped* out of sight but left her droppings in my studio, my place of creativity. Her dry, little droppings are easy to pick up, and not stinky, foul or messy. It was never in Molly's nature to leave a mess, so she must have had an urgent need to relieve herself. I wonder if she is *dropping* hints that I am not picking up.

Dream Actions

List the actions and activities in the dream.

WHAT IS HAPPENING:

The radio keeps playing the same program over and over again in a series of repetitive loops.

Molly is leaving droppings in my studio.

I confront my husband.

WHAT IS NOT HAPPENING:

I don't pick up the droppings.

I don't turn the radio off or change the channel.

I can't stop my husband from yelling.

DreamScapes

List the dream setting in your dream.

HOUSE:

    A house is a domestic dwelling for people who live together. It provides security, comfort, protection and shelter from the elements. Ideally, it is where one feels most content and safe, where one belongs. Home is where the heart is.

    In my waking life house, the upstairs is where I perform the supportive role of a dutiful and patient wife. The downstairs is where I am untethered and at peace in my art studio. A staircase connects the two stories of my life in this house.

    In my dream, the upstairs living room is shaking with the vibrations of an angry voice on the radio. Downstairs, there is a pile of dog shit on the floor of my studio. On the staircase in between the two stories, I confront my husband.

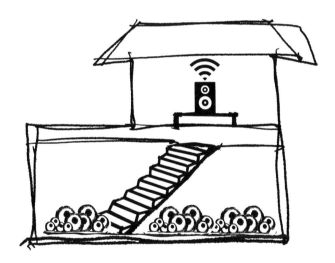

Questions

List a series of questions about the peculiarities in the dream.

Why has Molly come back from the land of the dead?
Why is Molly bigger and more beautiful than she was in her waking life?
Why has Molly left her droppings in my studio?
Were her droppings an accident?
Was Molly desperate to relieve herself?
Why didn't anyone listen to Molly's needs?
Why didn't I clean the droppings up before my husband found them?
Why didn't she shit in my husband's studio or in the living room?
Were her droppings left intentionally to send me a message?
Whose angry voice is being broadcast on the radio?
What program have I tuned into on the radio?
Why don't I turn the radio off or change the channel?
How do I know my husband has been yelling at my dog?
What would it feel like to stand up to my angry husband?
What would it be like if my husband could love me as much as Molly loved me?
What would it be like if I could love myself as much as Molly loved me?

Emotions

List the range of emotions stirred up by the dream.

In this dream, I feel so deeply euphoric that my beloved dog, Molly has returned. My heart feels so light. I feel so much love for Molly. I haven't ever had another companion with whom I shared such a strong emotional bond. I am flooded with sentimental nostalgia for happy days together.

In this dream, I feel the bottomless sorrow of deep grief for the loss of Molly. She has been dead and gone for so many years. I miss her presence in my life. I feel a deep longing to stroke her soft muzzle and belly. I yearn to look deeply into her loving eyes again.

In this dream, I feel outraged while the angry voice keeps repeating its relentless, soul-destroying fury. It permeates the atmosphere of my home with unending feelings of antagonistic condemnation.

In this dream, I feel overwrought with despair because my husband has no control over his anger. He is addicted to anger and will use any excuse to let it out. I feel so agitated that I blow up with my own pent-up anger.

In this dream, I feel deep remorse because I haven't taken care of my sweet pooch. I regret allowing my husband to hold any authority over her.

In this dream, I feel fury with all the angry men in my family for making me cower and cringe in corners like a dog.

In this dream, I feel exhausted by the ceaseless, repetitive, negative voices in my head and the tedious, redundant echo of my internal ire. I don't want to be an angry person.

In this dream, I feel empowered by my unleashed energy when I stand up to my husband and demand that he stop yelling. I feel bold and courageous.

In this dream, I feel hopeless when I realize that the bravery it took to confront the anger is meaningless. I feel subdued, diminished, defeated and worthless.

Memories

List a series of memories evoked by the dream.

I remember Molly, my sweet, shaggy, long-departed doggie. My faithful companion. She was always by my side. We were a team. I remember her eager, boundless energy, her utter joy in being alive. She loved me unconditionally with her whole heart and soul.

I remember my calm, private studio where I would go to be alone, to create my artwork in peace and to get away from my husband's field of energy.

I remember my living room where I would perform the duties of wife and homemaker.

I remember how I tiptoed around my husband on eggshells. I never challenged or defied his easily triggered rage.

I remember feeling trapped in a repetitive cycle of anger throughout my childhood and marriage.

I remember the voice of my father hollering in my childhood home and how he dominated the family with his bad temper.

I remember how my brother could control me with his hostility.

I remember my husband never scolded Molly in waking life…he only scolded me.

Molly DreamWriting

The Five Senses

Annotate the dream by activating it with an explosion of the senses.

Telltale Traces

MOLLY SPEAKS:

Since I have returned to Victoria's world, I have tried to get her attention in many ways, but apparently I'm invisible. I have no growl or yowl through which to make myself understood. I am boneless and barkless. So what can I do to get her attention? I feel a sense of urgency to get things out of my system. I can't hold back anymore. So I have shit on her studio floor to show her the crappy situation she is living in. But, hey, I haven't made a smeary, smudgy, lumpy, turdy mess. My droppings are tiny, compact, round and firm black pellets. They are not sloppy or squishy or formless. I have not splattered or dribbled all over. I haven't left a stinky, toxic mess. For goodness' sake, I have plunked my tidy turds on a drab old studio floor- a worn-out commercial vinyl with a flecked and marbled surface on which dirt isn't usually noticeable. If anyone else had shit on Victoria's studio floor, she would be disgusted by the mess, but she is never angry with me. If she had noticed my poop, she would have scooped it up, wiped the floor and let me out. But because her husband discovered my excreta, all hell has broken loose. Thanks to my little hints, Victoria can now see how dropping a few friendly turds on her floor has escalated into a nasty, foul tirade which is more toxic than any ol' pile of shit.

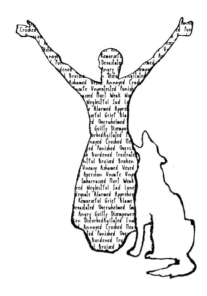

A Letter

Compose an emotive letter addressed to a dream entity.

MY DEAREST MOLLY,

    I'd thought I'd lost you forever.

    One day, we were happily frolicking in a farm field. You were tasting all kinds of strange things that you discovered, but within hours, you were writhing in death throes with a twisted stomach. I wasn't ready for you to die. You were the most loyal, loving pooch. We were counterparts. I felt like a part of myself was ripped apart. Now, you have returned as the ghostly doppelgänger of my living self.

    In my dream, I was careless with your complete trust in me. I should never have let my angry husband reprimand you. My heart is breaking, shattering, aching. How could I have allowed anyone to yell and scream at you?

    If I ask for your forgiveness, I know you will freely offer it to me with your unswervingly loving nature. But I can't forgive myself. I was so irresponsible and neglectful of your tender heart. Oh, my dear one, I am crying with remorse.

With deep regret,
Your Victoria

Deconstruction

Take apart your dream by breaking it down into a list of images.

MOLLY:
My dearly beloved, long-departed pet. My best friend and companion.
My soft, feminine, gentle, loving presence. My Soul Self

ALIVE AGAIN:
A return from the land of the dead.

UPSTAIRS, LIVING ROOM:
My conscious everyday waking world where I am a dutiful wife.

DOWNSTAIRS:
The depths of my unconscious dream world where my creativity thrives.

DROPPINGS:
A pile of shit. A persistent calling.

RADIO:
A Boom Box.

VOICE ON THE RADIO:
An accusatory, disparaging masculine invective.
A tumultuous, tempestuous, bellowing tirade.

ANGER:
Infuriation, vexation, denunciation.

HUSBAND:
My life partner. Habitual angry rage.

ACTION:
Recurring, repetitive cycles of blaming and shaming.

MY VOICE:
 An enraged war whoop. A battle cry.

I WILL FEED MOLLY:
 A vow, a promise, a sworn oath, a pledge of allegiance.

Reconstruction

Write another version of the dream without using the original vocabulary or wording.

A Shitty Situation

VICTORIA SPEAKS:
 My soft, feminine soul has been residing in the land of the dead for many, many years. Now, she has come home to me in the form of a gentle, loving presence who is calling to me from the depths of my unconscious dream world. But I don't hear her. I neglect her persistent calling. It has been so long since I have been companioned by the loving presence of my long-departed soul that I have forgotten how to listen to her voice.
 Meanwhile…
 A tempestuous, disparaging tirade is booming from a box with sounds of masculine infuriation bellowing with blame at an unseen female. I realize that this voice mirrors the habitual fury my life partner is inflicting upon my Soul Self.
 Suddenly…
 Something snaps inside of me. I become enraged. With a whooping battle cry, I rise up on behalf of my soul, for I am as innocent and undeserving of this anger as my poor defenseless pet.
 And yet…
 Despite my pledge of allegiance and my bravery, I have not stopped the attacks of blaming and shaming. The uproar of a reproachful invective continues to dominate my world. My Soul Self has departed and is nowhere in sight.

Harangue

Rip into an edgy dream image.

Beware Of The Dog

MOLLY GROWLS:

I hear your voice on the radio, but I don't see you. You are persecuting a creature who cannot fight back! Coward! Who are you? I'll tell you who you are! You are a savage monster protected by the anonymity of the airwaves! You are a shameless bully, a wrathful tyrant, a bruising goon, a habitual offender! You hide your true identity behind the airwaves to attack defenseless souls! You intimidate the vulnerable! You are an uncontrolled, unprincipled reprobate. But now you have stepped over the line, you brute. You've gone too far. Now you have attacked the very soul of the feminine spirit that I will protect with every fiber of my instinctive, animal rage. Come out and show your face, you tormentor! I am snarling, howling, roaring and riled up. I'm gonna tear you apart with my teeth. I'm gonna rip you from limb to limb. I'm gonna stop your heartless cruelty! Yowwwwwwwwl.

Molly DreamPoetry

Free Verse

A poem with no fixed rhythms or patterns of rhyme.

My Beloved Dog Returns

Molly has returned!
She is bigger,
and more beautiful
than when she was alive.

She hangs out
upstairs.
But she has left droppings
downstairs.

On the radio,
the voice of a man
brutally scolding
a dog,

and I know
my husband
has been scolding
Molly.

I confront him.
NO MORE!
He is not to yell at her
ever
again.

The next day
the radio voice
repeats.

A man's voice
brutally scolding
a dog,

and I know
my husband
has been yelling
at Molly.
Again.

BlackOut Poetry

Highlight the most compelling words and concise phrases in the dream.

Molly Dog Returns

My beloved dog Molly is alive again! She has returned to my home. She appears much bigger, more beautiful and hairier than she was in life. She has been hanging out with my husband and me upstairs in the living room… But she has been known to leave droppings downstairs in my art studio. Upstairs, I hear **an angry voice** on the radio screaming and **hollering** at a dog….Somehow I know my husband has been scolding Molly, again. I confront my husband. Sure enough, he admits that he has been yelling at Molly. He has been feeding her along with the cats, so he feels entitled to discipline her. For the first time in our marriage, **I stand up** to him. I tell him, from now on I will feed Molly and take care of her. He is not to yell at her ever again…. I think the matter is settled, but the following morning, I hear the same radio program repeating the angry voice over and over…. And I know that my husband has **ignored** me and is hollering at Molly again.

Ignored

An angry voice
hollering.
I stand up.
I am ignored.

List Poem

Begin each line with the same phrase "In this dream, I am…"

In this dream, I am Molly…
I am alive again. My feminine, animal spirit has been reborn.
I am a different, more beautiful version of my former self.

In this dream, I am The Radio…
I am a lifeless box endlessly broadcasting the voice of a powerful malevolent force.
I am programmed to fill the airwaves with the denunciation of the feminine spirit in the world.
I am a loud message repeating an unending loop that never stops.
I am an unyielding message that is always the same. I never change.

In this dream, I am a Pile of Shit…
I am no accident. I have transgressed the rules of proper decorum.
I am a messenger. I have appeared to disrupt the status quo.

In this dream, I am The Husband…
I am consumed by my temper
I am unaware of the psychic harm I inflict when I'm angry.
I am damaging my relationship with my wife.

In this dream, I am The Dreamer…
I am a different, better, stronger version of my waking self
I am here to save the day, to become the heroine of my story,
I am courageous and brave, but my actions are ignored.
I am wiped out, invalidated, and negated.

Ode

Draft a rhapsodic poem in the voice of a beloved dream character.

Molly's Ode to Joy

(Sing to Beethoven's Ode to Joy)

Oh, dream of joy! A Jubilee!
The land of living world, I see!
My eyes are bright, my gait unbound!
I am a very happy hound!

Is this my meadow, grove and lawn?
I romp and leap in fields 'till dawn!
Are these my whiskers, paws and tail?
I jump and run, my life regale.

Is this my ball? is this my bone?
Is this old sock my very own?
Is this my home? Is this my bed?
It feels like I was never dead!

Through veils of worlds, I come to stay
From far beyond the Milky Way
To join in life aglow, agleam
Oh, praise the glory of a dream.

Limerick

Contrive a humorous five line poem with a sing-song rhythm.

The Message

There was a poor doggie mistreated,
Whose toilette was far from completed;
She dumped poop near my door
Upon the smooth floor,
Her message, it seems, was excreted.

Pantoum

Form a repetitive poem building layers from recurring phrases.

Victoria's Remorse

Oh, Molly, what have I done to you?
I have neglected the urgency of your calling.
Faithful companion, you never left my side.
My heart cries out to you.

I have neglected the urgency of your calling.
Something is so deeply wrong.
My heart cries out to you.
Remorse cuts through me like a knife.

Something is so deeply wrong.
How could I let him yell at you?
Remorse cuts through me like a knife.
Brutal scolding, cruel recriminations.

How could I let him yell at you?
You cannot speak. You have no words.
Brutal scolding, cruel recriminations.
I must stop his endless rebuke.

You cannot speak. You have no words.
Faithful companion, you never left my side.
I must stop his endless rebuke.
Oh, Molly, what have I done to you?

Haiku

Design a three line poem to illustrate a moment of enlightenment.

Return

A return to life
A ghost from anger fleeing
A spirit broken

Ballad

Fashion a sentimental poem in four line stanzas.

The Husband's Ballad of Lost Love

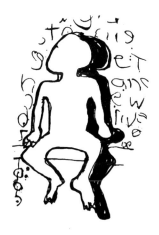

The color drained from out her face.
Her eyes like fires shone.
She cast a dreaded look at me.
Her heart had turned to stone.

She rattled, roared and swung her arms.
She argued wild-eyed.
Complaining of my tireless tongue.
No longer my sweet bride.

She clenched her teeth and hollered on.
No sound of wedding bell.
My heart it did explode with pain.
Our marriage gone to hell.

I find myself a soul in grief,
Remembering days of yore.
Before my heart was broken up.
Before her rage did pour.

Oh, dream! You are a callous thing,
In which I lost my wife.
You sent a sleep that troubled me
and changed my sorry life.

Oh dream! You are a callous thing,
In which I lost control.
You sent a sleep that troubled me
That slid into my soul.

The woman whom I loved so dear,
My wife, she was so mild.
I look upon those long-lost days
Before she was so riled.

My marriage once was sweet and pure
When we were bonded mates.
How could I think
that she'd explode?
Oh, sorrow is my fate.

Ditty

Make up a short comic rhyming poem for a child.

Ghost Turds

The turds were here, the turds were there,
The turds were on the ground.
And everywhere my pooch did go,
She left a tiny mound.

With lightweight thumps, those lifeless lumps
Did fall upon the ground.
But when they were discovered there,
She left without a sound.

In sharp rebuke, I shouted loud,
I caused a battleground,
Defending my sweet doggie,
But alas, my voice was drowned.

Lampoon

Devise a witty poem in couplets.

The Cat

Impervious cat
Intrinsically fat.
Choosing his spot
Not caring a jot.
Unflurried, unflustered,
Unruffled by bluster.
For trifles like that,
Who cares where he shat?
He can ignore
The frenzy and roar.
There's no yelling at
An oblivious cat.

Found Poetry

Craft an accidental poem formed from evocative text selected from magazines.

'place of suffering'

Maligned
accused
besieged
rattled by pressures
a struggle with in

Act now to prevent the next
TIME
Take care of the moment
more must be done to prevent
uncontained anger
gear up for A clash
demand safety

Get Results!

Molly DreamingArts

Storyboard

Sketch the dream story in panels.

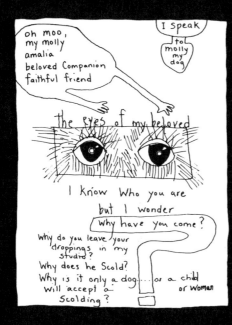

Zoom In / Zoom Out

Supersize and minimize the relationship between characters.

Mandala

Reimagine the dream as a model of symmetry.

Collage

Find pictures from magazines that express the feelings provoked by a dream.

Dream Map

Map out the dream with simple figures and geometric shapes.

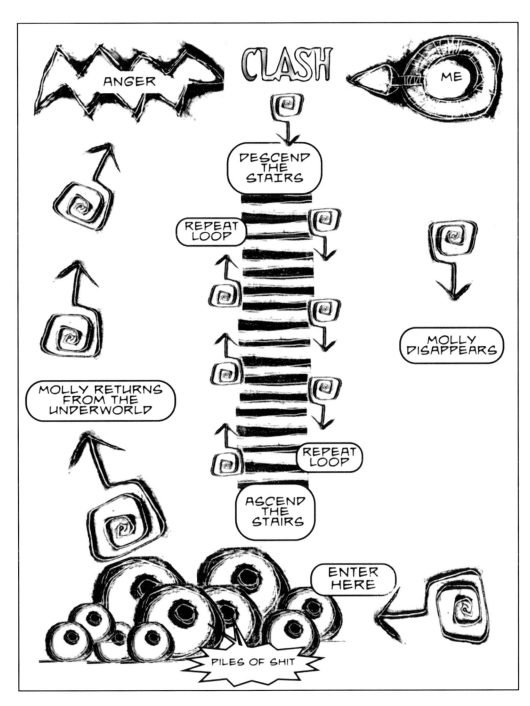

Diorama

Build a three dimensional scene in a container.

Mask

Fabricate a mask in the likeness of a dream image.

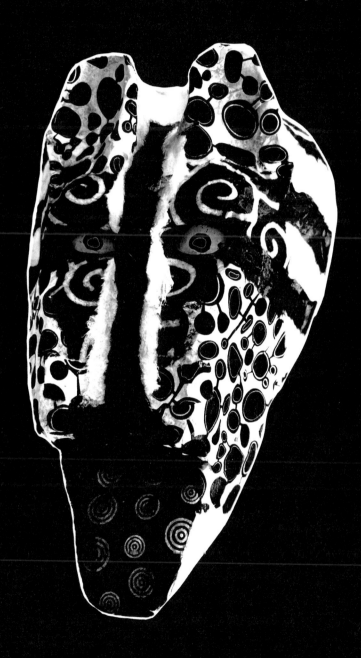

Painting

Enliven the dream's vitality with paint.

Molly DreamTheater

Monologue

Prepare a monologue from the viewpoint of a dream character.

Molly's Soliloquy of Long Lost Love

He never yelled at me in my life. He loved me, I know. And I loved him almost as much as I loved Victoria. We were so close, he and I. He took me adventuring. We went on hikes together. We scaled mountains. We swam in rivers. He loved me, I know. He yelled at Victoria, but he never yelled at me. And yet, now, in this dream, I feel the agony of injustice. He has treated me harshly. I am guilty. I admit it. I acknowledge the shitty situation that brought me under his lashing tongue. But his endless scolding will not clean up this mess. There must be another way.

Dialogue

Compose a character sketch between two dream beings.

The Scolding

HUSBAND SCOLDS MOLLY:
You are a bad, bad dog.

MOLLY CRIES TO MY HUSBAND:
Oh, please don't yell at me. Oh, please stop.

HUSBAND SCOLDS:
You have shit in my house. You know better. You are not acting like a well-trained, domesticated pet.

MOLLY CRIES:
I cringe with guilt over the mess I have made. I know I did the wrong thing, but I made as clean a mess as possible on an easy-to-clean floor. I made the mess in Victoria's studio, not yours. Victoria won't be very mad at me.

HUSBAND SCOLDS:
I set the rules for this household. I must be obeyed. I am furious because I have not controlled you and I won't stop hollering. You are bad, and I am mad.

MOLLY CRIES:
Please don't yell and scold. Please stop. I am cringing with guilt and remorse.

HUSBAND SCOLDS:
I can let my fury out on you because you cannot answer back. I know you will sit in fear and trembling because it is not in your nature to challenge or defy me.

MOLLY CRIES:
You are right. It is not in my nature to challenge or defy you. But it is in my nature to beg. Please stop. Your anger towards me hurts so deeply. It is so painful. All I want in life is to love fully and be loved in return. I don't want to be a bad dog.

Campfire Story

Turn the dream into a chilling ghost story.

The Ghost Who Scared The Crap Out Of Me

You might not believe this tale; maybe it's true, perhaps it's not. I don't even like to talk about it. It creeps me out. I don't even like to think about it… but I will….

[Pause with deep expectant breath]

In the wee hours of a dark and stormy night, the moonlight cast an eerie glow through the hallway of an old cabin as I tiptoed down the stairs.

[I glance and glare all around]

I lived in fear of a ghostly voice that haunted the top steps of that eerie stairwell. Whenever I let down my guard, there it was… Like the voice of a criminally insane monster ranting and raving, cursing and hollering.

[Audience hisses and boos]

Every night… I feared the angry voice thundering and rumbling and bellowing.

[Audience hisses and boos]

One day… I ventured along the creaking floorboards of the stairwell all the way down to the dark underground cellar. The reeking stench of putrefying, noxious dung wafted its way upwards into my old schnoz.

[Audience erupts with sounds of disgust]

Then…from somewhere deep within the dark cellar, I heard a voice sobbing, whimpering and whining. It was howling a woeful lament like an abandoned child… yearning for love… like a heart… breaking from neglect.

[I warble in an eerie ghostly child's singsong voice]
Where, oh where has my Molly dog gone?
Oh where, oh where can she be?
Oh, her fur is thick and her tail is strong,
Oh where, oh where can she be?

No answer came to my plaintive song. My heart went kathunk and kachunk. I summoned up all my bravery and searched for the source of the unearthly, phantasmic sound. I opened the portal very, very, very slowly. My skin prickled as the old cellar door opened with a loud creeeeeeeeak….I crept inside.

[My voice drops to a long drawn-out whisper]

And there it was…in the bowels…of the basement……..Masses… and Piles… of… Poop…! Ghastly… Dreadful… Appalling… Excrement was everywhere!

[Audience erupts with sounds of disgust]

My heartbeat erupted in horror….I felt the cold and clammy touch of fear…. I felt the air turn cold…

[I shiver]

Above me… a booming voice rose from the stairwell… a deafening, disembodied thunder like a volcano roaring and erupting with hot molten lava…

[Audience hissing and booing]

I became frantic. I yelled and hollered into the dark and stormy night. My voice burst defiantly from the bottom of my guts…
Ghosts Be Gone!

[Audience repeats Ghosts Be Gone! Ghosts Be Gone! Ghosts Be Gone!]

I yelled and hollered and screamed until, finally, the sunrise began to infiltrate the darkness. No other soul was around. I was entirely and utterly alone…. No more whimpering and whining…. No more woeful laments…. no more discontented, disembodied, grumbling ghosts…. No more volcanic booming voices….

[Audience responds with sighs of relief]

The ghoulish voices were all gone…. No ghosts…. No monsters…. The voices had vanished… but the Poop remained…. I was left staring at a pile of shit and inhaling a furry, doggy scent wafting in the air. I never did see the source of the voices above me or below me. The ghosts were all gone… Until the next night… I heard a simpering, whimpering voice softly chanting…

[I warble in a child's singsong voice]
Where, oh where has my Molly dog gone?
Oh where, oh where can she be?
Oh, her fur is thick and her tail is strong,
Oh where, oh where can she be?

…And the spectral phantom horror show repeated itself all over again… on and on… night after night.

[Audience hisses and boos]

Until one day… I took to covering the floors of the stairwell with eggshells so that I could train myself to walk very, very quietly so as not to disturb the sleeping ghosts.

[Audience makes shushing sounds]

And that is how I've lived since then… until this very day.

Wow, those ghosts sure scared the crap out of me!

[Audience hopefully explodes in applause]

Screenplay

Write a screenplay for a dream film or stage production.

WAITING FOR GODOG

(Based on *Waiting for Godot* by Samuel Beckett)

CAST OF CHARACTERS:

WIFEY: Protagonist: An exasperated woman

MASTER OF THE HOUSE: Antagonist: An angry man

DOGGIE: The Central Character: The faithful, female, canine companion of Wifey

ANGRY VOICE: The Herald: A booming disembodied male voice emanating from an old-fashioned radio

ACT ONE

Fade In:

Interior of a two-story house. Upstairs – Morning.

We open on a shabby living room without doors or windows on the top floor of a two-story home. We see an old-fashioned box radio sitting on a simple grey bureau.

ANGRY VOICE

The radio is broadcasting at full volume

BAD DOG! BAD DOG! BAD DOG! BAD DOG!

Cut To:

WIFEY

enters wearing a ratty, old chenille bathrobe.

She reaches out to change the channel

RADIO

emits an electrical shock

WIFEY

recoils

ANGRY VOICE

Booms from the radio's speaker

Only the Master of the House can change the channel.

Fast Fade Out:

End of the first act

MIDDLE ACT:

Fade In:

Interior of a two-story house. Upstairs - Afternoon

We open on the shabby living room without doors or windows on the top floor of a two-story home. We see the old-fashioned box radio sitting on a simple grey bureau.

DOGGIE

Sits cringing beside her food bowl

ANGRY VOICE

The radio is broadcasting at full volume

BAD DOG! BAD DOG! BAD DOG! BAD DOG!

MASTER OF THE HOUSE

enters bellowing and raging loudly

BAD DOG! BAD DOG! BAD DOG! BAD DOG!

WIFEY

Enters wearing a superwoman costume

Upon witnessing the abuse, she shrieks over The Angry Voice and the Master of the House

DON'T EVER YELL AT DOGGIE AGAIN!

Silence ensues.

Polychromatic Lights fan out over the scene.

WIFEY

stands tall with arms crossed in a superwoman pose.

She smiles triumphantly and croons to Doggie

GOOD DOGGIE, GOOD DOGGIE, GOOD DOGGIE, GOOD DOGGIE

Slow Fade Out:

End of middle act

FINAL ACT:

Fade In:

Interior of an art studio. Downstairs - Evening

We open to an art-filled studio with a boarded-up door on the ground floor of a two-story home. Colorful paintings are on the walls. Books fill the shelves. A rocking chair is facing the boarded-up door.

ANGRY VOICE

The radio is broadcasting at full volume

BAD DOG! BAD DOG! BAD DOG! BAD DOG!

WIFEY

enters wearing a sagging superwoman costume.

She is alone. Her head is hanging down. Her shoulders are slumped. She reaches out to turn the radio off.

RADIO

emits an electrical shock

WIFEY

recoils

ANGRY VOICE

Booms from the Radio's speaker

Only the Master of the House can turn the Radio off.

WIFEY

slumps into the rocking chair and stares out toward the boarded-up window.

Fade Out:

End of the Last Act

The play ends because there is nothing to be done, nowhere for Wifey to go and no way to change the outcome.

Song

Shape song lyrics into a soulful dream ballad.

My Sweet Molly Lament

Sung by Victoria to the tune of "The Streets of Laredo"

As I climbed up from my studio downstairs,
As I walked into my parlor one day,
I heard a voice booming, all angry and bitter,
All chiding and blaming and cruel as doomsday.

I sensed from this tumult my mate had been shouting.
His words he did blast as I boldly walked by.
I spied my dear doggie all furry and shaggy,
All cowed in a corner, rebuked by this guy.

It was once in the garden she used to go dashing;
It was once in the garden that she used to go play.
But she took a big shit where she shouldn't have aught to.
Got caught in reproach 'cause she would not obey.

Oh, beat a drum slowly and growl a tune lowly.
I played the dead march as I sang her this song.
I went to her garden and laid her poop deeply,
For she was a smart doggie and knew she'd done wrong.

I loved my sweet Molly, so sweet and so winsome.
I bitterly wept as I sang my sad song.
Before I returned home, her soul had departed.
I loved my sweet doggie, although she'd done wrong.

Body and Soul

Animate a dream entity through rhythmic movement.

Melodrama

Invent a humorous dream play with an improbable plot and exaggerated characters.

A Shaggy Dog Story

A BELLIGERENT BROADCASTER enters upstage right:
   With a voice like the tempestuous tone of tyrannic terror and a treacherous, tumultuous, turbulent tongue, a monstrous, menacing, misogynistic meat-eating miscreant is yelling at a cardboard cutout of a cringing, cowering dog.

BAD DOG! BAD DOG! BAD DOG!

A COURAGEOUS CRUSADER enters downstage left:
   With a cold, controlled, combative, cascading voice, the Courageous Crusader wields a burst of bold Brobdingnagian bravery against outlandish, overwhelming odds.
In short, she is infuriated, incensed and irritated!

STOP YELLING AT MY DEVOTED, STEADFAST, FAITHFUL, LOYAL HOUND DOG! YOU MEAN MISERABLE MISCREANT!

Wheezing with insufferable innuendo, the Belligerent Broadcaster continues wrathfully raving with blistering, bristling, antagonizing authoritarianism.

BAD DOG! BAD DOG! BAD DOG!

With a hot voice roaring like bitter, boiling water, the Courageous Crusader becomes riled, enraged, resentful… and acutely annoyed.
In short, she is horribly, hopping mad!

STOP YELLING AT MY DEVOTED, STEADFAST, FAITHFUL, LOYAL HOUND DOG, YOU MEAN MISERABLE MISCREANT!

A SANGUINARY SYCOPHANT enters from a trap door in the stage floor:
   Filled with the provokingly paranoid, post-industrial, argumentative anxiety of the

misdirected, modern-age male, the sycophant is contentious, cross, cranky, crazed and quarrelsome. He joins the Belligerent Broadcaster with uncontrolled, undisciplined, unfettered outbursts in the relentlessly, unruly, unrestrained refrain….

BAD DOG! BAD DOG! BAD DOG!
BAD DOG! BAD DOG! BAD DOG!

AN ANGELIC ANIMAL APPARITION is lowered onto center stage from the catwalk.
   A phantasmagoric, psychopompic, poltergeistic pup sits astride a cutout plywood cloud suspended high above the actors on the stage. A deficatious dump of doo-doo is dropped on the bombastic, belligerent broadcaster and his savage, sadistic, sanguinary sycophant. A profuse pile of shockingly shitty shit inundates the stage and incapacitates the two vile, vicious, villainous varmints.

The BAD DOG refrain fades out, and a moment of silence ensues, followed by a chorus culminating in a crowning climactical crescendo of sweet-sounding, symphonious serenades of happy hallelujahs and hosannas.
   As the curtains close, the cutout plywood cloud lifts the courageous crusader and the angelic animal apparition into the heavens as the two unite in euphoric, exhilarating ecstasy.

Molly DreamJourneys

Fairy Tale

Transpose the dream into a fairy tale.

The King Shit of Turd Mountain

Once upon a time, there was a Wrathful, Angry, Jealous King. He hated everyone in the kingdom who loved The Exceptional, Exuberant Queen. For this reason, he kept The Queen locked up in the tower so she could never befriend or love anyone else but him. He had a magic spell cast around her tower so that no one but he could enter, and The Imprisoned Queen could never, ever escape.

Day and night, Malicious Winds and Malevolent Voices swirled around her tower door like invisible, menacing spirits. They were so fierce they could destroy any Knight in Shining Armor who came to rescue The Imprisoned Queen.

Then one day, it came to pass that a Phenomenal, Phantasmic Phantom vaulted over the guardhouse, over the moat and over the drawbridge into the great hall of the castle to liberate The Imprisoned Queen. As The Phantom lunged towards the castle stairs, The Wrathful King became enraged. He ran after her with his Iron Dagger of Ill Temper. The Phenomenal, Phantasmic Phantom escaped The King's pursuit by leaving A Prodigious Pile of Foul, Fetid Excrement at the foot of the stone tower steps. This load of shit was so thick that no mortal could pass over it for a hundred years.

No longer impeded by the King's pursuit, The Phenomenal, Phantasmic Phantom leaped up the tower steps to Rescue the Queen. The Malicious Winds and The Malevolent Voices swirled around the tower with a Mean-Spirited Mystical Magic that no human hero could endure, but The Phenomenal, Phantasmic Phantom could not be destroyed because she was not a member of the human race. She nimbly approached The Queen's bedchamber door where The Lonely, Imprisoned Queen felt her loving presence radiating throughout the tower. But alas, whenever The Imprisoned Queen tried to open her tower door, the Mean-Spirited Mystical Magic prevented her from escaping. In spite of her royalty, The Queen was only human. She could never, ever escape from the spell of The Malicious Winds and The Malevolent Voices.

And so it came to pass from that day forward that The Phenomenal, Phantasmic Phantom lay beside the Imprisoned Queen's door at the top of the cold, stone castle stairs. And although the Queen couldn't see or touch her, she knew the Fabulous Phantom was there beside her. The Queen remained imprisoned, but she was never ever lonely again.

From that day forward, The Prodigious Pile of Foul, Fetid Excrement remained at the foot of the cold, stone tower staircase. The Angry King could nevermore scale the steps that led to his Queen. He never realized that The Pungent Pile of Foul, Fetid Excrement would turn into a Prodigiously Profuse Pile of Gleaming, Gilded Gold if only he released the Mean-Spirited Mystical Magic over The Queen. He could have become the wealthiest King in all the land. But he never released The Imprisoned Queen, so he never discovered the fabulous fortune that lay right under his nose.

And so it came to pass that The Wrathful, Angry, Jealous King lived out his wrathful, angry, jealous life alone, trapped forevermore in his castle filled with The Pungent Pile of Foul, Fetid Excrement as the King Shit of Turd Mountain.

Moral

If you get shitfaced over an overprotective, jealous love, you will end up living alone in a house full of shit.

Board Game

Turn the dream into a game.

When the Shit Hits the Fan

A game for two consenting married adults on the brink of divorce.
The goal is to play the game once and never play it again.

The Rules of the Game:
- Each player chooses a husband or wife wedding cake figure as a playing piece.
- Reward, penalty and wild cards are shuffled and placed face-down on the edge of a spiral-shaped playing board.
- Each player draws a card, takes a turn, and then follows the directions provided on the card to determine his or her movement on the board.
- The game is lost if the "Shit Hits the Fan" card is pulled.
- The game is won if the "Unconditional Love" card is pulled.
- The first player to win or lose shouts, "No More!"
- The board is tipped over and tossed away, never to be played again.
- Penalties will apply if the same married couple plays the same game again.

Reward Cards: Dog Cards

- Well Behaved: Slide two squares in any direction
- Needs a Walk: Advance four steps
- Needs to Be Fed: Stand still
- Needs a Hug: Return to the safety zone
- Faithful: Jump five squares ahead
- Needs Attention: Pick another card
- Needs to Be Groomed: Pass GO
- Eager to Please: Jump forward to the opposite player's square
- Unconditional Love: The game is won

Penalty Cards: Shit Cards

- Shit a Brick: Move one square back
- Get Shit-Faced: Move two squares back
- Full of Shit: Do not pass GO
- Step in a Pile of Shit: Forfeit a turn
- Don't Know Shit: Lose two turns
- Shoot the Shit: Slide backward
- Beat the Shit Out: Go to jail
- Shit Your Pants: Go back to square one
- No Shit: Get bumped off the board
- Give a Shit: Go to the safety zone
- Take a Shit: Take another card
- Shit Hits the Fan: The game is lost

Wild Cards: Cat Cards

- Impervious: Move one square in any direction
- Shameless: Move anywhere on the board
- Aloof: Curl up and take a nap
- Oblivious: Play some other game

Comic Strip

Copy clipart to portray characters and scenes from the dream story.

Alice in Dreamland

Invite Alice to fall into the dream as an impartial observer through the dreamscape.

Recalcitrant Noncompliance

Awakened by the patter of thumping paws and a softly burbling bark, Alice jumps to her feet. She sees the whiffling of tail and whiskers of an elusive MollyWock continually appearing and disappearing in the distance. Alice follows a trail of droppings which leads to a giant checkerboard upon which chess pieces are bellowing and bawling in a disorderly fashion.

BLACK KING: [Shouting at the top of his lungs]
    Bad MollyWock! Bad MollyWock! Bad MollyWock!

ALICE: [Timidly approaches His Majesty the Black King]
    Would you tell me, Your Royalness, why you are so annoyed with the MollyWock?

BLACK KING: [In a nasty temper]
    Hold your tongue, child. Don't interrupt me! I'm going to tell you all her faults. The MollyWock is guilty of insubordination, rebelliousness and non-compliance with the Rules of the Game. She is a BAD MollyWock! She ought to be ashamed of herself. She must be punished.

ALICE:
    And why are you so angry with the White Queen?

BLACK KING: [Irascibly, waving his vorpal sword all about]
    Fiddlesticks! I am NOT angry; my game is just different from the Queen's game. She is a most provoking thing.

In confusion and bewilderment, Alice backs away from the Black King.

Alice approaches Her Majesty, the White Queen.

WHITE QUEEN: [Shouting at the top of her lungs]
    Off with his head! Off with his head! Off with his head!

ALICE: [Timidly approaches Her Majesty the White Queen]
If it pleases Your Majesty, tell me why are you so angry?

WHITE QUEEN:
Well, it doesn't please me, you young whippersnapper. Who are you, child? What could you possibly want here?

ALICE:
My name is Alice, may it please Your Majesty. I am curious about this peculiar game you are playing,

WHITE QUEEN:
I am the only one with the proper skills and talent to control this game, but I am constantly being thwarted by my annoying consort, the King, and the piles of excrement around the board. "Off with his dominating, infuriating head!" I scream. But how can I behead His Royal Highness when I know all his frumious henchmen will come after me with their vorpal swords? There is no possible way an innocent little girl like you could ever understand how difficult it has become to play this foul, nasty grownup game. No matter how long I play, I can never seem to win.

Still confused and bewildered, Alice backs away from the irascible Black King and the uffish White Queen and cautiously approaches the MollyWock.

ALICE:
You look like such a fine beast with such a mimsy tail and such long whiskers. Why have you left your slithy droppings around the Queen's playing field?

MOLLYWOCK:
Why, to get her attention, of course!

ALICE:
But your method is so mischievous and naughty.

MOLLYWOCK:
Yes, it is. The Queen has been too busy commanding and demanding indulgences from her royally annoying Black King to notice me. She looks straight through me as if I were a ghost.

ALICE:
But you are a ghost!

MOLLYWOCK:
All the more reason to invent a way for the Queen to notice me.

ALICE:
So you choose to pester Her Royal Majesty, The Queen, with your stubborn infractions of the royal rules?

MOLLYWOCK:
My recalcitrant noncompliance with the rules of the game is necessary. If Her Majesty The Queen can't manage my behavior, she will have to reconsider the strategy of the game she is playing. She will have to devise new rules.

ALICE: [Looking reproachfully at the MollyWock, speaking in as cross a voice as she can muster]
Oh, you wicked little thing! Really MollyWock, the Queen and King taught you better manners. You ought to know better; you know you ought. The King was so angry, MollyWock, when he saw all the mischief you have been doing, he very nearly knocked you out of the game, and you would have deserved it, you mischievous little darling.

Alice grasps the MollyWock by the scruff of her neck and gives her a little kiss to make her understand that she is in disgrace.

Mythic Journey

Transform the dream into a legendary adventure.

The Sisyphean Sorrow of Sisters

Whimpering beside the entrance to the land of the dead, the spirit of the long-departed sylph, Amalia mourned the loss of her past life. She petitioned the god of the underworld for a chance to be reunited with her beloved sister Nymph, Viktorjia in the world above.

But Viktorjia had bathed in the river of forgetfulness and oblivion. She had forgotten her long-lost sibling Amalia after being given in marriage to a bad-tempered Titan. Descended from a long line of dethroned former gods, the entire dynasty of infuriated fathers, disempowered sons and ballistic brothers sought to rule the heavens above and dominate the world below without a drop of kindness. To survive the wrath of the Titans, Viktorjia disguised herself as an obedient, mortal woman without memories of happier times. She submitted her will to the domination of generations of belligerent Titan fathers, Titan brothers, Titan uncles and Titan sons. Day in, and day out, they stormed through her palace with their booming thunderbolts. Her home shook with quaking, shuddering tempestuousness exploding with the sound of their clashing tridents. Viktorjia had fallen on sorrowful times.

Meanwhile, her steadfast sister, Sylph, Amalia, continued to petition the god of the underworld to allow her to return to the land of the living. At long last, he granted her wish. But as with all gifts from the gods, there was a catch. She could return to the land of the living, but she would remain invisible. Amalia was so ecstatic about her return that she did not pay attention to the terms and conditions required.

When the spirit of Amalia arrived in the land of the living, she wept upon realizing that she could not be seen. Her dark tears transformed into tiny black droppings that were scattered at Viktorjia's feet. Viktorjia recognized the droppings as the tears of her long-lost beloved sister, Amalia. Her memory of happier times was restored.

Viktorjia knew that Amalia had returned but couldn't find her anywhere. She searched and searched. She listened for Amalia's footsteps, but the clashing of tridents and the smashing of thunderbolts throughout the palace prevented her from hearing any footfall. The sorrowful Viktorjia pleaded with the Titans to silence their thunderous activities, but her pleas fell on deaf ears.

The heartbroken Amalia was sent back to the underworld without ever being seen by her grieving sister, and Viktojia remained caught in her mortal form, trapped in a Sisyphean loop of sorrow throughout the rest of eternity.

Child's Play

Speak about the dream with a tender childhood voice.

I Want to be a Good Doggie

Victoria's Infant Self Speaks:

My Daddy's ill-tempered voice booms and bellows all around the house. His venomous tongue-lashing fills the air.

My Mommy tries to stop My Daddy from blowing a fuse, but My Daddy's loud ranting and raving just keeps going on and on. He uses bad language like the words "crap." I crap in my diapers, but Mommy doesn't seem to mind that very much. It is the word "crap" used in insulting sentences that upsets her. He scares the crap out of me when he threatens to beat the crap out of her.

My Mommy and My Daddy love dogs, so in order to be a Good Baby, I try to behave like a Good Doggie so they will love me.

My Brother loves to hear the expletives in the hallways of our house. He loves to make My Daddy holler. He loves to see My Mommy cry. He is a very Nasty Baby. He doesn't care about making My Mommy or My Daddy happy. He behaves like a Bad Doggie all the time.

I can't seem to stop the noise by behaving like a Good Doggie. I can't stop My Brother from behaving like a Bad Doggie. I can't make My Mommy happy. I can't stop My Daddy from scaring the crap out of me. I don't have control over my poop or anything else. I am powerless to change my world.

Portrait of Power

Reflect upon themes of power and powerlessness in a series of dream collage tableaux.

A SHOCK TO THE SYSTEM

Anger has been controlling my life and the lives of so many others around the world. I have watched how women are controlled by rageaholic lovers; families are ruled by menacing alcoholic fathers; societies are threatened by fundamentalist proselytizers; masses are manipulated by vengeful conspiracy theorists and governments are overrun by power-seeking politicians.

I feel powerless. I have not been able to stop the repetitive cycle of abuse both in my personal life and in relation to the issue of women's rights across the globe. It is time to fight back!

A NEW STRATEGY FOR FIGHTING

I have been holding on to the notion that women have to fight fire with fire; the only way to conquer anger is with more anger. There has to be another way to find my personal power. It's time for me to surrender my attachment to anger.

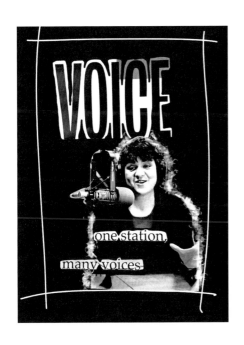

VOICE: ONE STATION, MANY VOICES

I live in a world culture that transmits patriarchal contempt toward women over the airwaves. I want to switch to a channel that broadcasts the voices of women raised in songs of power, freedom and love. I do not need to turn the radio off; I need to change the station.

SUPERHERO RISING

I feel confidence rising within me! I am confronting the unrelenting energies that have kept me from blooming into my fully realized Self. I am filled with inner and outer strength! I feel the awakening of my potent, vital, superpower spirit! I will never be the victim of masculine rage again! I am ready to stand up for myself and all women with soul power.

Pandora's Dream Box

Place synonyms for the negative dream emotions in a box and glue antonyms in the lid.

Pearl of Great Price

Meditate on a way to turn the affliction in the dream into a treasure of great value.

A Pearl of Wisdom

DEAR MOTHER OF PEARL,

Recurring themes of tyranny and intimidation have gotten under my skin. I have had these unrelenting narratives inside my tender shell for many years. In my defense, I have deposited layers of resentment and aggravation around my heart. I have paid a high price to become a second-rate common cultured pearl. But I no longer want to pretend to be a faultless gem of womanly perfection.

I petition you to pry dreams of unconditional love from the depths of my soul. Let new deposits of loving kindness surround me as I meditate on my dream of Molly's Return. Help me to turn layers of self-protection into luminous pearls of wisdom. Transform my hardened heart into an authentic pearl.

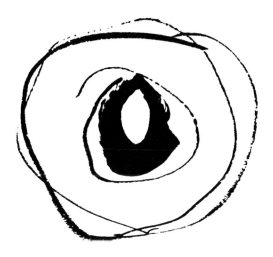

Witches' Brew

Concoct a witches' brew of magical protection from toxic feelings in the dream.

Bitch's Brew

Preparation:

    Soak the hair of a dog that bit you in a base of oil and water.
    Flavor with insoluble deadly nightshades.
    Add fermented, raw nerve endings from the spine of a rabid mongrel.
    Drop in an essential trace element of resentment.
    Whisk in a pinch of salt extracted from the tear ducts of a very small mouse.
    Mix relentlessly with bad blood and dry rot.
    Thicken with bitter herbs and a generous amount of acid rain.
    Bring to a roiling boil.
    Cook this concoction over an open flame for a year and a day.
    Simmer every night thereafter to maintain a venomous potency.

Prescription:

    Whenever an angry confrontation occurs:
    Dilute this concoction with pure spirits to avoid a severe burning sensation in the heart and a cramping in the gut. Condense it into a homeopathic reduction until not even a single molecule of the original noxious brew remains.

Dosage:

    To erase all repetition of this nightmare's morbific derangement, administer a heaping tablespoon of this dilution in a very large cup of spirits as often as necessary.

A New Ending

Bring the dream forward.

Another Outcome

A raging, ranting, raving radio voice is being broadcast at top volume throughout my home. I reach out, turn the radio off, and yank the plug out of the socket. I confront my husband and tell him in no uncertain terms that he has scolded this sweet nature for too long. He is never to yell at Molly or me ever again. I march down the stairs. I wipe the shit off the floor. I call to Molly. She comes to me with her tail wagging expectantly and her leash in her mouth. Together, we go for a walk. A long walk. We never return to this house filled with anger.

Labyrinth

Meditate on recurring dream patterns that reflect waking life.

The Heart of the Matter

I enter the labyrinth with the provocations of The Molly Dream on my mind. As I switch back and forth, I change direction between the two halves of my consciousness. In one direction, I walk with my inner antagonist, the angry one who is dictatorial, demanding, hypercritical and judgmental. In the opposite direction, I walk with my guardian spirit, Molly, who is peaceful, compassionate, imperturbable and forgiving. By the time I reach the center of the labyrinth, I know it is time to stand up to the angry shadows I have harbored within. It is time to treat my Soul Self with the unconditional, loving compassion I have experienced through my love for Molly. I retrace my footsteps to the entrance of the labyrinth having changed direction. The time has come to own and accept The Molly Dream messages dropped from my night mind to reveal that the unrelenting enemy is within me. The repressive one is not my husband nor my father or brother or uncles, but my own punishing inner voice. It is time for a reversal on my path from inner blame to inner compassion.

Utopian Vision

Rewrite the dream by turning every dark dream image to light.

A Journey Together

I hear a tranquil voice on the radio, tenderly singing to a dog, and somehow I know my husband has been together with Molly since her return to our home. He has been crooning sweet nothings to her as he feeds her and snuggles with her. The next morning, I hear a joyous rhapsody playing on the radio, and I know that my husband has joined me in the delight of Molly's return. I clean the whole house, top to bottom, while singing the melody to my sweet gentle doggie and dancing with my sweet, gentle spouse.

For too long, I've been focused on Anger. I have forgotten about the power of Love. Life should be a journey of the heart. In marriage, a husband should be a devoted, attentive companion, not a scorn-filled adversary. On the world stage, masculine and feminine energies should be supportive and compassionate, not hostile or antagonistic.

Sanctuary
Visualize a place of refuge and serenity

Prayer

Ask for divine intervention to replace the personal turbulence in the dream with universal peace and compassion for all living souls.

A Supplication for All the World

Oh, Divine One, I beseech you,
Hear the cry of my soul for all women who suffer as I have suffered.
Hear my cry for all women who are oppressed;
for all women who are mistreated;
for all women who are negated;
for all women who need protection;
for all women who yearn for peace;
for all women who hunger for love.
Break down the walls of tyranny.
Burn away our rage.
Shelter our spirits.
Restore our souls.
Surround us in the embrace of compassion.
Divine One, hear my prayer
for all women who suffer as I have suffered.
Give us the strength to change our world.

It's not the shit we face that defines us; it's how we deal with it.
   Ahmed Mostafa

The Molly Dream Revisited

A New Dream

"Molly Dog Returns" seemed like such a small, simple dream, just a dream about a man yelling at a dog. In waking life, my husband had yelled at me the day before. It would have been easy to dismiss this dream as mere day residue because it never occurred to me how deeply I was affected by my husband's outbursts. I never acknowledged that this atmosphere of anger in our marriage kept me disengaged and disembodied. I was accustomed to a lot of hollering in my childhood home, so my husband's behavior was mild compared to that of my tempestuous father and brother. Unlike them, my husband was never menacing or cruel. And I had compassion for him. I believed he could not help himself from sudden episodes of impulsive anger. He suffered greatly from his childhood with a verbally abusive father. I always found a way to excuse his extreme behavior and repeatedly forgave him. I believed that his anger didn't affect me. He could not control himself, but I could control myself. I thought I could handle it. Whenever he spun into a rage, I would simply check out. I would watch him rave from somewhere outside myself. I was so focused on my husband's affliction that I couldn't admit that my soul was being assaulted.

Through engagement with my dreams, I was able to experience numerous shifts in perspective regarding the real issues beneath my waking struggles. When I began to see the Molly dream as a metaphor for my life, the trajectory of my life changed. Taking responsibility for myself and my own anger, I unwittingly uncovered the path to liberation. I moved away from old patterns of blaming all the bad-tempered men in my life. I gave voice to all that was pent up inside. I played with my inner tricksters and danced with my devils. I practiced standing up to the antagonistic men in my life. I came to understand that the voice of anger is just a voice; it had no actual power over me. I converted my bitter, internal monologue of self-sacrifice and self-loathing into self-acceptance and self-respect. I unearthed pearls of wisdom and seeds of compassion. I found profound inner healing by touching my wounds.

Through my conversations with Psyche, I experienced the enormous power of dreams for personal catharsis. Before I opened up the "Molly Dog Returns" dream, the notion of self-love was a cliché New Age concept. Yet, when I read back words of unconditional love written from a dog's perspective, I learned that fierce self-love is not only admirable but also attainable. As I worked through the Molly dream, I gained a true understanding of what it means to experience unconditional love. I was able to experience the absolute truth of it.

Many years after the Molly dream, after many setbacks and delays, I began the final version of this book. Then this new Molly dream came…

Molly Dog Returns Again

Molly is with me!
We are together on a journey.
We look into each other's eyes.
Although we have been traveling together for a long, long time,
She apologizes for not being attentive.
No, Oh No, I say.
I am the one who has not been attentive.
All is forgiven.
We hug and embrace.
We look into each other's eyes with total lucidity.
We are back together again!
She is beautiful!
Her coat is smooth and sleek!
She leaps and runs!
She is her joyous, doggy self!

Contemplation

On my journey, I am accompanied by what I thought was dead in me. I look deep into the eyes of Molly. I see my reflection. I reconnect with my Soul Self. We are one again. I am filled with the presence of spirit. After being inattentive to my book writing, all is forgiven. I am writing again with a rush of pure joy. I have begun to integrate the Molly Dream into my book. The work has embraced me. I am filled with clarity. I feel the warm embrace of my Soul aligning my inner journey with my book journey, at last.

The Inner Journey

The dialogue between the ego and the Self creates the Soul....
It changes life from a meaningless puzzle into an awesome journey.

Marion Woodman

When I first embarked upon my journey into the depths of the dream world, I had no idea of the immensity inside me. But by tending to my dreams, my limited sense of self unraveled. I discovered that I am far more mysterious and multi-dimensional than I had imagined. The underworld is boundless, with an infinite variety of life forms dwelling below the surface.

Many of them, it turns out, have my face.

This excavation introduced me to a new sense of myself. What began as a tentative experiment evolved into a deep affinity and lifelong practice. My dreams ignited a spark in me and fueled my work. I found my authentic, creative voice. Introspective dream journaling revisioned my story. Dream by dream, I have woven a bold new narrative for my life.

AFTERWORD

Source of Creativity

When you do things from your soul, you feel a river moving in you.

Rumi

After writing, crafting and performing your way through this book, in whole or in parts, you have tasted the intoxication of the DreamingArts. Your familiarity with the language of dreams has grown broader with ever-widening spheres of interpretations and associations. You have stood at the intersection where chaos and madness meet. You have forged past impassable barriers, changed directions, made decisions and confronted your fears and joys with profound levels of insightful, heartfelt inner wisdom. Your dexterity with juicy writing, dramatic performances and inspired artwork has matured and ripened. Your dream journal is filled with passionate poetry and perspicuous, pellucid prose. You have written fairy tales embroidered with hyperbole, and foolish limericks embellished with bombast. You have sung new songs and told tall tales. Your journal is warped with paint, sticky with glue and stained with tears of poignancy and pathos.

Released from rational, reductive thinking, you have harnessed the non-ordinary imaginal realm. Your dreamwork has transformed into mind-bending, hair-raising, rip-roaring, heart-stopping creative growth. The truth of who you are has been ingested and integrated into your heart, mind and body. The DreamingArts has poured forth a rich and vibrant portrait of your soul.

EPILOGUE

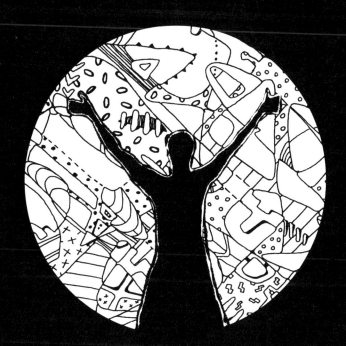

APPENDIX A

Ethics Statement from the International Association for the Study of Dreams (IASD)

"The International Association for the Study of Dreams recognizes and respects that there are many valid and time-honored dreamwork traditions. We invite and welcome the participation of dreamers from all cultures. There are social, cultural, personal and transpersonal aspects to the dream experience.

IASD celebrates the many benefits of dreamwork yet recognizes potential risks. IASD supports an approach to dreamwork and dream sharing that respects the dreamer's dignity and integrity and acknowledges the dreamer as the decision-maker regarding the significance of the dream. Systems of dreamwork that assign authority or knowledge of the dream's meanings to someone other than the dreamer can be misleading, incorrect, and harmful. Ethical dreamwork helps the dreamer work with their dream images, feelings, and associations and guides them to more fully experience, appreciate and understand the dream. Every dream may have multiple meanings, and different techniques may be reasonably employed to touch these multiple layers of significance.

A dreamer's decision to share or discontinue to share a dream should always be respected and honored. The dreamer should be forewarned that unexpected issues or emotions may arise during the dreamwork. Information and mutual agreement about the degree of privacy and confidentiality are essential in creating a safe atmosphere for dream sharing.

Dreamwork outside a clinical setting is not a substitute for psychotherapy or other professional treatment and should not be used as such."

The International Association for the Study of Dreams is a non-profit, international, multidisciplinary organization dedicated to the pure and applied investigation of dreams and dreaming. Its purposes are to promote an awareness and appreciation of dreams in both professional and public arenas; to encourage research into the nature, function, and significance of dreaming; to advance the application of the study of dreams; and to provide a forum for the eclectic and interdisciplinary exchange of ideas and information.

www.asdreams.org

APPENDIX B

DreamingArts as a Therapeutic Tool for Psychotherapy

Giving a dream to a Jungian analyst is a little bit like feeding a complex quadratic equation to someone who really enjoys math. It takes time. The process itself is to be savored. The solution is not always immediately evident.

Sara Corbett

All of us are healthy enough to practice creativity. It is not a dangerous endeavor requiring trained facilitators; however dreamwork outside a clinical setting is not a substitute for psychotherapy or other professional treatment. Although DreamingArts activities may feel therapeutic, they should not be undertaken lightly. Be cautious about doing this work alone, for there are potential risks. You will come face to face with old, toxic patterns, dysfunctional habits, jealousies and prejudices. You may require a guide to find healing in your nightmares and difficult dreams. It is essential to be mindful of your mental state and reach out for support when needed. If you have experienced abuse, violence or addiction, it is not advisable to follow this path without professional help. However, a DreamingArts practice can be a profound tool for collaboration with a psychotherapist and, when brought into a therapeutic setting, can enhance and expand inner work for both client and therapist.

A conscientious professional DreamWorker will help you by being a guide, not a self-styled oracle. Beware of dream practitioners who might try to assume authority over your dreams' meanings. Hotshot DreamWorkers can amaze you with cleverness and dazzle you with quick-witted interpretations. But they can also mislead you with inaccurate and damaging assumptions. In the long run, they can take the juice out of your journey. A single spin, given to you by a "dream expert," excludes other possible pathways to meaning. Your dream can become frozen like a fossil, encased eternally in amber. An ethical DreamWorker will lead you to experience the dream by guiding your associations and remaining open to multiple explanations. Remember, the final authority about the meaning of your dreams is always you. Be prepared to reject notions that don't resonate within your core of knowing. Look for a therapist who encourages your self-expression and who will coax out your own insights in your own words. Your practice in DreamingArts can be a valuable complement to augment professional guidance in depth psychology or spiritual direction.

APPENDIX C
Resource List For Further Reading

Aizenstat, Stephen. *Dream Tending: Awakening to the Healing Power of Dreams.* Spring Journal, 2009.

Barasch, Marc. *Healing Dreams: Exploring the Dreams That Can Transform Your Life.* Riverhead Books, 2000.

Barrett, Deidre, ed. *The Committee of Sleep: How Artists, Scientists, and Athletes Use Dreams for Creative Problem-Solving—And How You Can Too.* Crown Publishers, 2001.

Berry, Walter. *Drawn into the Dream: How Drawing Your Dreams Can Take You to the Land of Awes.* Los Angeles: Precocity Press, 2021.

Bly, Robert. *A Little Book on the Human Shadow.* HarperOne, 1998.

Bosnak, Robert. *A Little Course in Dreams: A Basis of Jungian Dreamwork.* Shambhala, 1988.

Cassou, Michele. *Life, Paint and Passion: Reclaiming the Magic of Spontaneous Expression.* TarcherPerigee, 1996.

Corso-Steinmeyer, Bambi. *DreamTracking: Track Your Dreams and Transform Your Life.* Self Published, 2021.

Delaney, Gayle, Ph.D. *All About Dreams: Everything You Need To Know About Why We Have Them, What They Mean, and How to Put Them to Work for You.* HarperOne, 1998.

Epel, Naomi. *Writers Dreaming: 26 Writers Talk About Their Dreams and the Creative Process.* Vintage Books, 1994.

Faraday, Ann. *Dream Power.* Berkeley Publishing Group, 1997.

Fontana, David. *The New Secret Language of Dreams: A Visual Key to Dreams and Their Meanings.* Chronicle Books, 1994.

Freud, Sigmund. *The Interpretation of Dreams.* Avon Books, 2019 (Reissue Edition).

Garfield, Patricia. *Creative Dreaming: Plan and Control Your Dreams to Develop Creativity, Overcome Fears, Solve Problems, and Create a Better Self.* Simon & Schuster, 1995.

Goldberg, Natalie. *Writing Down the Bones: Freeing the Writer Within.* Shambhala, 2016.

Gover, Tzivia. *Dreaming on the Page: Tap into Your Midnight Mind to supercharge Your Writing.* The Collective Book Studio, 2023

Hoss, Robert J., Robert P. Gongloff, and Stanley Krippner, eds. *Dreams that Change Our Lives.* Chiron Publications, 2017.

Johnson, Robert A. *Inner Work: Using Dreams and Active Imagination for Personal Growth*. Harper & Row, 2001 (reprint).

Jung, C.G. *Dreams*. Routledge Classics, [year], 2nd Edition.

Kamenetz, Roger. *The History of Last Night's Dream: Discovering the Hidden Paths to the Soul*. HarperOne, 2007.

Kaplan-Williams, Strephon. *Dreamworking: A Comprehensive Guide to Working with Dreams*. Journey Press, 1991, (Out of Print).

Klerk, Machiel. *Dream Guidance*. Hay House Publishing 2023.

Lipsky, Jon. *Dreaming Together: Explore Your Dreams by Acting Them Out*. Larsen, 2008.

McCloud, Scott. *Understanding Comics: The Invisible Art*. William Morrow, 1994.

Mellick, Jill, Ph.D. *The Art of Dreaming: Tools for Creative Dream Work*. Conari Press, 2001.

Metzger, Deena. *Writing for Your Life: Discovering the Story of Your Life's Journey*. HarperOne, 1992.

Mindell, Arnold. *Working with the Dream Body*. Lao Tse Press, 2001

Schiller, Linda Yael. *Modern Dreamwork: New Tools for Decoding Your Soul's Wisdom*. Llewellyn, 2019.

Tanner, Wilda. *The Mystical, Magical, Marvelous World of Dreams*. Sparrow Hawk Press, 1988 (Out of Print).

Taylor, Jeremy. *The Wisdom of Your Dreams: Using Dreams to Tap into Your Unconscious and Transform Your Life*. TarcherPerigee, 2009.

Taylor, Jeremy. *Dream Work: Techniques for Discovering the Creative Power in Dreams*. Paulist Press, 1983.

Ullman, Montague. *Appreciating Dreams: A Group Approach*. Sage Publications, 1996.

ONLINE RESOURCES

Comic book style: plasq.com

Images: images.google.com

Free dictionary: www.thefreedictionary.com

Thesaurus and word tools: Word Hippo at www.wordhippo.com

Rhyming dictionaries: www.rhymezone.com, www.rhymer.com

Urban dictionary: www.urbandictionary.com

Acknowledgments

This book would not have been possible without the dedication of students, colleagues and chosen sisters who have generously shared their dreams, hearts, minds, and unending, enthusiastic support for this book. Special thanks to Freya Diamond, Gail Rieke, Alex Fischer, Jean Stratton, Judythe Sieck, Maggie Tomei, Nancy Paap, Jeannette Scott, Johanna Vedral, Regina Klein, Nancy Grace, Susan Hill, Althea Brimm, Bridget Flanigan, Diana McKevilly, Micki Halloran, Rhonda Noble, Jeannette Scott, Susan Hill, Sr. Miriam Randall, Julie Kuck, Victoria Hughes and so many more.

I am grateful to fellow writers whose shoulders I have cried upon and now stand upon; Malka Drucker, Katherine Leiner, Lauren Schneider, Walter Berry, Naomi Epel, Tzvia Gover, Johanna Vedral, Linda Yael Schiller, Marta Aarli, Bambi Corso, Justina Lasley, Kelly Sullivan Walden, Makenna Goodman and Mark Lewis Wagner.

I am indebted to my teachers: Dr. Eric Craig and Dr. Stephen Aizenstat, my psychotherapists Martha Davis and Alicia Lauritzen; and the authors who inspired my ideas and artwork: C.G. Jung, Joseph Campbell, James Hillman, Fritz Perls, Marion Woodman, Robert Boznak, Jon Lipsky, Robert Johnson, Wilda B. Tanner, Rodger Kamenetz, Clarissa Pinkola Estés, Deena Metzger, Michele Cassou, Anne Lamott, Mark Kistler, Scott McCloud, Julia Cameron, Natalie Goldberg.

Grateful acknowledgment goes to the annual conferences of The International Association for the Study of Dreams (IASD) - a multidisciplinary organization dedicated to the pure and applied investigation of dreams serving as a forum for the eclectic and interdisciplinary exchange of ideas and information. Over the past thirty years, I have had the honor of meeting and studying with master practitioners, mentors, and colleagues in this esteemed organization: Gayle Delaney, Jeremy Taylor, Deirdre Barrett, Robert Hoss, Jean Campbell, Lee Irwin, Roberto Gongloff, Richard Wilkerson, Clare Johnson, Laurel Clark, Linda Yael Schiller, Sheila Asato, Daniel Deslauriers, Montague Ullmann, Robert Van de Castle, Patricia Garfield, Fariba Bogzaran, Rita Dwyer, Robert Waggoner, Johanna King, Richard Russo, Katherine Bell, Scott Sparrow, Lana Nasser and many more.

I want to express my sincere appreciation and high praise for my editors and coaches - all book magicians who helped me restructure this book with patient, perceptive suggestions, observations, provocations, encouragements and guidance. Ariella Robbins who named this book; JoAnne O'Brien-Levin, who organized thirty years of workshop notes and selected the dreams that tell the story of my struggle to write this book; Wayne Lee who raised the cutting room floor to eye level and inspired me to anchor each of the projects and activities with the Molly dream example; Julie Simpson who challenged and reformed my style and intent while wrestling with my elliptical modes of expression, run-on sentences, and excessive use of adjectives and semicolons. Ann Lowe, who helped me envision a thematic strategy for the illustrations throughout the manuscript; Judythe Sieck, who lent her artful calligraphy to the cover; and expansive accolades to Peggy Pfeiffer and Gabriele Morwinski of BadDog Design, who tirelessly honed and shaped the final layout for this book with the spirit of generous collaboration.

Special thanks to my German language translators Johanna Vedral and Janina Pollak, my Spanish language translator Elizabeth Garay and my Italian language Translator Marzia Bosoni who deciphered my words with sensitivity through their exceptional language skills.

Many thanks to my late mother, Eve Rabinowe, and my former husband, Aku Oppenheimer, for their endless encouragement toward my creative endeavors.

Additionally, I would like to extend a heartfelt recognition for years of design inspiration and graphic experimentation to Gina D'Ambrosio and Esperanza Zane. And above all, my most profound appreciation to my "Little Sister" Sean Wells for years of creative innovation, technical assistance, steadfast motivation, and guidance. Many of her graphic designs from my first book, *I Had the Craziest Dream Last Night*, are incorporated into the illustrations for this book.

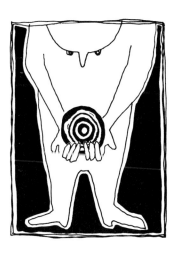

About the Author

Victoria Rabinowe is an American artist, author, international educator and director of the DreamingArts Studio in Santa Fe. She has led dream groups, workshops, seminars and retreats at her DreamingArts Studio in Santa Fe, on Zoom and abroad for conferences, universities, museums, writing schools and art academies. She has taught thousands of psychotherapists, spiritual guidance counselors, educators and creatives worldwide to understand the language of dreams through poetry, prose and book arts. She is educated at Harvard, Boston Museum School, Emerson and Pacifica Graduate Institute. Her artwork has been exhibited across the globe. Victoria lives in a tree house in an urban forest above her DreamingArts Studio in the artists' colony of Santa Fe, New Mexico.

A DreamingArts Workshop is a creative adventure like no other!
To learn about DreamingArts Workshops, Seminars and Retreats visit
www.VictoriaDreams.com.

Made in United States
North Haven, CT
10 June 2024

53448796R00179